MATTHEW, THE FIRST EVANGELIST:

A Reader's Commentary on the Gospel According to Matthew

Ben Johnson

MATTHEW, THE FIRST EVANGELIST:
A Reader's Commentary on the Gospel
According to Matthew

Scripture quotations are from *Today's English Version*.

ISBN 0-89536-286-4   PRINTED IN U.S.A.

For our children —
Samuel
Jennie Ruth
Krister
Jesse

TABLE OF CONTENTS

Matthew 1 7

Matthew 2 18

Matthew 3 26

Matthew 4 30

Matthew 5 35

Matthew 6 43

Matthew 7 50

Matthew 8 56

Matthew 9 61

Matthew 10 68

Matthew 11 73

Matthew 12 78

Matthew 13 85

Matthew 14 94

Matthew 15 98

Matthew 16 103

Matthew 17 107

Matthew 18 112

Matthew 19 118

Matthew 20 124

Matthew 21 128

Matthew 22 135

Matthew 23 141

Matthew 24 146

Matthew 25 157

Matthew 26 155

Matthew 27 165

Matthew 28 173

Matthew 1

Matthew 1:1

[1] This is the birth record of Jesus Christ, who was a descendant of David, who was a descendant of Abraham.

This Gospel is the only one to begin with Jesus' family tree on the human side. (Luke eventually gets around to it in his third chapter.) By this beginning, Matthew already reveals his own respect for tradition and for family.

Jesus' family connections are indeed impressive. From Abraham he inherited a willingness to follow God's call in directions not fully clear in the beginning; from Jacob an ability to converse easily with God; from Ruth an ability to trust; from David the gift or poetry; from Solomon the gift of wisdom; from Hezekiah a concern for the law of God; from Zerubbabel a desire to build up; from Joseph manual skills; and from his mother faith.

Yes, Jesus was heir to a great family. And he was heir in the same way that every Jew in his day was heir to that particular list of great ones. In that the list traces the descent to Joseph — and Jesus was not the natural son of Joseph — he was heir by adoption and not by blood line.

Of course it can be argued that Mary's blood line was every bit as impressive as that of Joseph. And it probably was. It is not given in the Bible; in fact, one does not even know the name of her parents.

But the Jews of Jesus' day were not worshipers of blood lines. Ruth was not a Jew. It was possible for a person to become a Jew by circumcision or to be automatically recognized as a Jew by being born to a Jewish mother.

So the record is a geneaology of Jesus through his step-father.

The two figures emphasized are David and Abraham. By raising these up for emphasis, Matthew reveals a twin aspect of Jesus' career. He is the chief man of faith and the chief man of government. Many a young man and woman of conscience have trouble deciding whether to seek to better the world through religion or law. Martin Luther started out as a student of law, but shifted his sights to a life in religion. Yet his own career meant as much for the governments of Europe as it did for the religious life of the time.

Abraham is remembered as a person of faith. He is the single person with whom God started after the disappointments of the time of Noah and the tower of Babel. And Abraham, impressive as he is for his ability to trust God and strike out alone, is a hero of faith.

1:2-6a

[2] *Abraham was the father of Isaac; Isaac was the father of Jacob; Jacob was the father of Judah and his brothers. [3] Judah was the father of Perez and Zerah [their mother was Tamar]; Perez was the father of Hezron; Hezron was the father of Ram; [4] Ram was the father of Amminadab; Amminadab was the father of Nahshon; Nahshon was the father of Salmon; [5] Salmon was the father of Boaz [Rahab was his mother]; Boaz was the father of Obed [Ruth was his mother]; Obed was the father of Jesse; [6] Jesse was the father of King David.*

The marvel of Abraham is that he could take God at his word, and believe. It was the high God who was speaking to him (Genesis 12:1-4). Such an event is easier to believe as a part of the biblical record than it was for Abraham when it happened to him. Abraham could have simply said: "I must have eaten something that didn't agree with me."

Recently a young seminarian found his seminary studies grinding to a standstill. He was having trouble thinking of Jesus as God, and preferred to think of him simply as a man whose purpose it was to teach people how to get along in this world. But he also found this proclamation empty and unsatisfying.

Six months earlier while lying on his bed, he had seen a man who looked like Jesus walk out of his closet, walk over to where he was lying, look down at him and shake his head as if to say "What a shame!" and then walk back into the closet.

This young man said to himself: "I probaly caused that to happen. If that was Jesus, why wasn't his complexion darker?" In this and similar ways he convinced himself that Jesus had not appeared to him.

What if Abraham had done the same thing? What if he had been one of the multitude of people in the modern world who deny to God the power to speak either through the Scriptures or through his own presence? Many contemporary scientists and theologians deny God's ability to call out his own in any generation. Many preachers spend more time undermining than mining the Bible. Humankind seeks to wrest control of life itself from God through abortion, mercy killing, and machine-sustained unconscious life.

Abraham himself has been subject to the challenge of biblical skepticism. Recent discoveries of archives in the Middle East have turned up the name Eber (Genesis 11:16), perhaps the same as Abraham's ancestor. Two hundred years of radical criticism have heightened the reality of biblical figures as real citizens of a cosmopolitan world little different from our own.

Abraham was different from most cosmopolitans of our day in his willingness to believe this strange God who called him. And he was to follow this God through his life, in a mission which was nothing short of religion-founding.

1:6b-11

[6b] *David was the father of Solomon [his mother had been Uriah's wife]; [7] Solomon was the father of Rehoboam; Rehoboam was the father of Abijah; Abijah was the father of Asa; [8] Asa was the father of Jehoshaphat; Jehoshaphat was the father of Joram; Joram was the father of Uzziah; [9] Uzziah was the father of Jotham; Jotham was the father of Ahaz; Ahaz was the father of Hezekiah; [10] Hezekiah was the father of Manasseh; Manasseh was the father of Amos; Amos was the father of Josiah; [11] Josiah was the father of Jechoniah and his brothers, at the time when the people of Israel were carried away to Babylon.*

Abraham is also a person with feet of clay. Four thousand years seem as the day before yesterday when one sees him in Genesis 12:10-20 deceiving the Pharaoh by claiming that his beautiful wife, Sarah, was his sister. A young couple trying to break into the pop music world of New York have learned the same trick. If the husband introduces himself as husband, he finds that the music people have no interest in his wife's musical ability. But when he introduces himself as her brother, the music and his wife get a great deal more attention. But it is for them, as it was for Abraham, a dangerous game.

Abraham, who was willing to follow God anywhere, did not believe that God could protect him from the Pharaoh. A few centuries later the Israelites were to learn about the power of God over the Pharaoh. But it can be seen in this story that the greatest biblical heroes can also be examples of unfaith.

The other person held up as a special model for Jesus is King David. Jesus is not simply a person of faith. He is also a political man, a descendant of the King and a new King. This role of Jesus means that the church is always in tension with government. Separation of church and state is a position of the United States Constitution. It is not a position of Christianity. The placement of David as the main model for Jesus is based upon his Kingship.

This placement means that Christianity is a political movement. Many Christians resent this fact about Christianity. Christians who have forgotten that Christianity is political have stood by while millions of Jews were killed in Europe. Christians who have forgotten that Christianity is political allowed the enslavement of black Africans in this country.

But to say that Christianity is political does not say that Christians must always be on the liberal side of a question. It also does not say that all Christians will be on the same side of a question. But it does say that followers of a King and members of a Kingdom will be concerned and involved in the ordering of life in this world.

David was a King who not only ruled but who also poured his life into the nation of Israel. When the armies of Israel were stymied by the Philistine champion Goliath (1 Samuel 17), it was David who had the courage to go out in single combat against this nine foot giant. When the King needed music, it was David who played. It is David who is remembered as the writer of great psalms. It is he who sought to provide a place of worship for the God of Israel. He was one who sought to lead at every level of the life of his nation.

1:12-16

[12]After the people were carried away to Babylon: Jechoniah was the father of Shealtiel; Shealtiel was the father of Zerubbabel; [13] Zerubbabel was the father of Abiud; Abiud was the father of Eliakim; Eliakim was the father of Azor; [14] Azor was the father of Zadok; Zadok was the father of Achim; Achim was the father of Eliud; [15] Eliud was the father of Eleazar; Eleazar was the father of Matthan; Matthan was the father of Jacob; [16] Jacob was the father of Joseph, the husband of Mary, who was the mother of Jesus, called the Messiah.

Like Abraham, David was not always successful in his undertakings. A wandering eye led him to steal the wife of another man (2 Samuel 11) and arrange to have that man killed in battle. He paid for this act by God's taking from him the child born to him and Bathsheba. His beloved son, Absalom, raised a rebellion against him (2 Samuel 13). He was not allowed to build a temple to God. An important lesson of the life of David is that he paid for many of his sins by punishment in his own lifetime. Yet God continued to love him and to promise that his family would stay on the throne.

Two facts emerge from this double ancestry of Jesus. He would be a man of faith and a King. He did come preaching not an earthly kingdom, but the kingdom of God — a kingdom not simply political but not non-political. On this subject more will be said later. Here it is just to remember both Abraham and David.

Second, there is common ground between David and Abraham. They were both men alive in the world. They labored, married, had children, suffered, died. They did not shrink back from life and they did not come through life without disturbing anyone or anything. That could

not be said of these men upon whom God placed his hand.
They remained people of faith and people alive in the
world. They were both central figures in God's plan. But
they did not walk on egg shells. They pushed forward
into a future that neither knew, but from which neither
shrank.

1:17

*[17] So then, there were fourteen sets of fathers and sons from
Abraham to David, and fourteen from David to the time when the people
were carried away to Babylon, and fourteen from then to the birth of the
Messiah.*

The ancient world loved numbers. The western world
knows little of the special quality of numbers. But both
the Ancient Chinese and the Hebrews believed that the
understanding of numbers offered a route to an
understanding of people and the world. Both the Hebrew
and the Greek languages used the same symbols for
letters and numbers, just as Latin used its letters for
numbers. (What time is it when it is XII o'clock? The
answer is not that it is XII o'clock, but that it is 12
o'clock.) The western world has taken its numbers from
the Arabic language, therefore it is difficult for
westerners to see the connections between letters and
numbers.

The most famous New Testament reference to a
mysterious number, the unraveling of which reveals
heavenly secrets, is the passage in Revelation 13:17-18,
where the number of the beast is said to be 666, which is
to be sufficient to identify the character. A book of the
same period called the Apocalypse of Enoch includes
detailed number speculation, as does the Jewish
Philosopher Philo, a contemporary of Jesus.

Thus it is that Matthew notes that there are **fourteen**
generations from the first patriarch to the great king,
fourteen from David to the end of the monarchy and the
exile to Babylon, and **fourteen** from the exile to the new
Davidic King Jesus. And in this way Matthew reveals his
understanding of the time of the working of God prior to
Jesus.

1:18-21

[18] This was the way that Jesus Christ was born. Mary his mother was engaged to Joseph, but before they were married she found out that she was going to have a baby by the Holy Spirit. [19] Her husband Joseph was a man who always did what was right, but he did not want to disgrace Mary publicly, so he made plans to divorce her secretly. While he was thinking about all this, an angel of the Lord appeared to him in a dream and said: "Joseph, descendant of David, do not be afraid to take Mary to be your wife. For the Holy Spirit is the father of her child. [21] She will give birth to a son and you will name him Jesus — for he will save his people from their sins."

The appearance of Jesus Christ in this world began with a miracle, the wonder of the virginal conception of Jesus in the womb of Mary prior to her marriage to Joseph. It is not surprising that such a thing should happen. The biblical record is full of miracles. A story which ends with a resurrection from the dead could be expected to begin in an unusual way.

Yet the birth of Jesus from a virgin is a story that many serious modern Christians have trouble believing. Perhaps they have known too many brides whose first child came early, even though the others all took nine months. It seems easier for some to believe that nature took its course a little early than that the Holy Spirit caused this pregnancy.

Others point to the fact that neither the Gospels of Mark and John nor the Apostle Paul mention the virgin birth of Jesus. If this were really true, they say, would it not have been more widely known and mentioned in early Christian literature?

But such arguments do not hold water. More remarkable is the fact that Matthew and Luke agree on the fact that Jesus was born of a virgin, even though they do not in common report much other data prior to the beginning of Jesus' ministry. The literary evidence argues for the virgin birth, not against it.

That the story confronts the reader with a modern situation is revealed by the reaction of Joseph. He knew that he was not the father of the child. And that must have meant that Mary had been fooling around. Her infidelity freed him from his promise. It did not occur to him that there was another answer to the question.

Nothing less than the intervention of an angel was necessary to change Joseph's mind. The angel came in a dream with a four-fold message. First, the angel confirmed that the child that Mary was to have was indeed by the Holy Spirit. Second, Joseph should continue in his plans to marry Mary. Third, the child would be a boy. And fourth, he should be called Jesus.

Angels do not appear often to mortals. When they do appear it is normally to bring a message that humans would not normally conclude from the testimony of their senses. Sometimes they appear in dreams, as here, sometimes by day or night to people fully awake, as in the case of the angel(s) at the tomb of Jesus. Sometimes they are visible to mortals while they are celebrating (so Luke 2:14).

The word angel is Greek for messenger. These are the same beings referred to in the Old Testament as the sons of God or the heavenly hosts. Some modern people have trouble understanding the existence of angels because they think that the only living beings in God's great universe are humans and animals. More to the point, many secular people do not believe that any being can exist apart from the body.

But the ancients knew, and the Bible reflects that knowledge, of the existence of levels of being. The 82nd Psalm reflects a knowledge of gods subordinate to the high God. The sixth chapter of Genesis reflects an involvement of the sons of the gods with the daughters of men. The book of Job knows of a Satan who wanders to and fro upon the earth. The letter to the Colossians (1:16) bears clear testimony to the existence of these immaterial beings who are also creatures of God.

While moderns have had difficulty understanding, or even allowing this invisible realm, recent researches into reports of people who have experienced clinical death have accustomed people to thinking again about the soul apart from the body. The language employed by people in describing their experiences sounds remarkably like Paul's description in 1 Corinthians 15:35-58 of the spiritual body.

It is from this spiritual realm that the angel of God comes. God's angels perform various tasks for him. There are messenger angels and guardian angels. There is a great realm of spirit from which came Elijah and Moses to communicate with Jesus. There is also, of course, the realm of evil spirits, presided over by Satan himself. The spiritual world has as many possibilities of good and evil as has the material world.

The angel breaks in with news that Joseph would not have concluded from the evidence of nature. In the birth of Jesus, God himself has intervened directly. Virgin birth is not an ordinary event. But it was the way God chose to act.

In verse 21 the very purpose of Jesus is revealed. He would be many things — teacher, healer, miracle worker. But his purpose, that inherent in his name, is deliverance from sin. This theme recurs in this Gospel.

1:22-25

[22] Now all this happened in order to make come true what the Lord had said through the prophet: [23] "The virgin will become pregnant and give birth to a son, and he will be called Emmanuel" [which means, "God is with us"].

[24] So when Joseph woke up he did what the angel of the Lord had told him to do and married Mary. [25] But he had no sexual relations with her before she gave birth to her son. And Joseph named him Jesus.

Matthew understands that the Bible is the charter of salvation. The simple appearance of an angel could be a delusion. The devil too has angels. Paul knew this when he said in Galatians that another gospel should not be believed even if it were preached by a heavenly messenger.

But the combination of the biblical witness and the testimony of the angel is mutually supportive. The Bible is full of accounts of encounters between God and humans. It is from such stuff that primary religious experience is made. But the Scriptures are the record of God's activity with his people over a long period of time. First Israel. Then the early church. Matthew does not simply appeal to the angel's testimony, he also searched the Scriptures. There he found in a prophet hundreds of years before an indication of this event (Isaiah 7:14).

Much has been written on the subject of the Old Testament as it relates to the appearance of Jesus Christ. Opinions range from the idea that everything about Jesus was foretold, to the notion that Old Testament books deal only with their own time and do not anticipate the coming of Jesus.

What needs to be seen is that every biblical book spoke to its own age, it points to Jesus Christ as the center point of God's working, and it points to every age. When the prophet Isaiah offered the words of Isaiah 7, he likely understood the prophecy himself as relating to an event soon to come in his own time. But the nature of prophecy is not that it is carefully constructed by the prophet. It is revealed to him. And words revealed by God for the near future would have also been shaped with Jesus in mind.

The word virgin in this text in Isaiah need not mean that a virgin birth was necessarily expected. The word translated virgin can also mean "young woman." It is in the actual event of Jesus' birth that one learns that it was a virgin birth. That is, New Testament facts help to understand Old Testament prophecy.

Most clearly one can see the priority of the actual event over the prophecy in the name given to the baby. The Isaiah passage gave his name as Immanuel. The angel said he should be called Jesus. When the baby was named, it was at the command of the angel and not on the basis of Isaiah. But Isaiah helped the people understand that this birth was of God.

Joseph acted upon the angel's word. How much greater this world would be if more people were obedient to heavenly commands. He also followed the heavenly command in the matter of the name. The new baby would not bear the name of David or Moses, which were the two most famous names in Israel's history. His name was not unique, however. He shared it with the famous assistant to Moses, Joshua. Joshua in Hebrew is the same as Jesus in Greek.

In one respect, however, Joseph acted on his own. Matthew reports that he and Mary did not live as man and wife until after the birth of Jesus. No doubt this decision on his part grew out of his respect for the wonderful way Mary had come to bear this child. Joseph must have been a genuinely God-fearing man, quite an appropriate person to help raise Jesus to adulthood.

Matthew 2

Matthew 2:1, 2

[1] Jesus was born in the town of Bethlehem, in the land of Judea, during the time when Herod was king. Soon afterwards some men who studied the stars came from the east to Jerusalem and asked: [2] "Where is the baby born to be the king of the Jews? We saw his star when it came up in the east, and we have come to worship him."

The men who studied the stars are astrologers. The country of their origin is not mentioned; but Persia is considered likely, in that in Persia, astrology had reached a high art.

Astrology proceeds on the assumption that all of the cosmos is one inter-related unit. The stars themselves and the planets are understood to reflect — indeed to presage — events and personages on earth. Judaism and Christianity have often been suspicious of astrology, not because they do not believe that it can accurately reflect events in the world, but because people who depend, upon astrology may end up worshiping the creation rather than the Creator.

That is quite a different objection from the one that the modern scientific community raises against astrology. Scientists of the type who recently signed an appeal to the population to reject astrology would be equally opposed to prophecy, or to the power of God to intervene in the affairs of humans.

People of biblical faith understand that the whole world is God's. It is a world in which he hung a rainbow to indicate that he would not send another flood (Genesis 9:15). It is a universe in which he placed the stars (Genesis 1:14-18). It was one of these stars, perhaps hung by God at the beginning of time, which the eastern astrologers saw.

The astrologers knew this star to be linked with the destiny of the Jews. They went to the city of the Jews to inquire further what this might mean. The technical expression used is "we have seen his star in the ascendancy." They understood that this meant that the future would turn on this figure. And as readers of the signs of the times, they wished to offer him worship.

2:3-5

[*3*] *When King Herod heard about this he was very upset, and so was everybody else in Jerusalem.* [*4*] *He called together the chief priests and the teachers of the Law and asked them, "Where will the Messiah be born?"* [*5*] *"In the town of Bethlehem, in Judea," they answered. "This is what the prophet wrote:*

Herod was greatly disturbed by this turn of events. The throne which his father had schemed to gain him, and which he had secured in Rome, in battle, and with the taking of much blood, now was threatened from a new side.

The limits of astrology when compared with the Bible are clearly indicated in verse 4. While the astrologers could find Jerusalem, they needed more accurate wisdom to bring them to the place where this King would be born. Here the supremacy of Scriptures was revealed. It was to the interpreters of the Jewish Scriptures that Herod turned. Because it was from the Jews that salvation comes, and while distant astrologers could read the heavens, they were not blessed with the Bible of the Jews.

2:6

[*6*] *'You Bethlehem, in the land of Judah,*
    Are not by any means the least among the rulers of Judah;
    For from you will come a leader
    Who will guide my people Israel.' "

The prophecy is found in Micah 5:1-4. It is another reminder that a search of Holy Scriptures produces results. Again, an ancient prophet is a key to events that were to come hundreds of years later.

The prophecy itself points to a little town five miles to the south of Jerusalem. It is nothing by comparison to the great city, Jerusalem. But it has a place in the plan of God.

Micah goes on to tell two more facts about the Messiah. He would be a shepherd. And he would be a man of peace. The first fact is amazing in that shepherding was not an admired profession. But it is to be remembered that King David had been a shepherd for his father's flocks when he was a boy. But to call this new leader to emerge from Bethlehem a man of peace, is striking. David had been a man of war. Any person who could displace Herod and the Romans would be expected to be a warrior. Would it mean that he would be a man of peace?

2:7, 8

[7] So Herod called the visitors from the east to a secret meeting and found out from them the exact time the star had appeared. [8] Then he sent them to Bethlehem with these instructions : "Go and make a careful search for the child, and when you find him let me know, so that I may go and worship him too."

Herod acted upon the basis of the combined information he gathered from the astrologers and the biblical scholars, like many a crafty leader, that put him in control of more information than anyone else in the situation. He shared his information with the astrologers, and sent them the five miles south to the little town of Bethlehem.

But even in a little town, finding a baby would be a problem. Herod the King urged them on, with the promise that when they found this baby, he would join them in worship.

2:9-11

[9] With this they left, and on their way the star appeared — the same one they had seen in the east — and it went ahead of them until it came and stopped over the place where the child was. [10] How happy they were, what gladness they felt, when they saw the star! [11] They went into the house and saw the child with his mother Mary. They knelt down and worshiped him; then they opened their bags and offered him presents: gold, frankincense, and myrrh.

Here the story changes significantly. Up to this point the astrologers and students of the Bible were reading signs already a part of the furniture of the universe. But a star millions of miles away that can perch directly over a little house in a little town is no longer a clue of

astrology. It is the direct leading by the hand of God to
the place where Jesus and his mother were.

"How happy they were,
What joy was theirs
When they saw the star!"

In telling the story, Matthew broke into verse. The
astrologers began to comprehend the power of God only
when they moved those five miles from Jerusalem to
Bethlehem. Instead of distant calculations, there was
now a star to lead them. An old friend, but this time a
nearness that allowed for no miscalculation.

They enter the house (v. 11). Matthew reveals no
knowledge of a manger. The child was born in the house
of his own parents. When they entered they knelt and
worshiped Jesus. They did not mix up the bearer and the
born. As amazing as a virgin birth was, it did not lead to
the worship of Mary. But it was to Jesus, the new King,
that proper obeisance was offered.

The worship of the astrologers was followed by gifts
of material value. They brought gifts fit for a king. It is
worthwhile noting that the fact that they brought gifts
points to the confidence they had that they would find
him.

The astrologers are never said to be three in number,
as the song has it. The number is perhaps a natural
surmise from the three gifts.

2:12
[12] *God warned them in a dream not to go back to Herod; so they
went back home by another road.*

Herod never received the astrologers' report. Again
God intervened in human history. He warned them not
to return to Herod. Through God's intervention the
astrologers were enabled to live to a ripe old age. Herod
would no doubt have demanded that he be taken to the
place of the babe. And had he found him, it is sure that he
would have attempted to kill him. The astrologers would
either have been killed or have been unwilling
accomplices in the death of the new king.

All of this was averted, however, because on divine warning, the astrologers never returned to Jerusalem.

2:13-15

[13] After they had left, an angel of the Lord appeared in a dream to Joseph and said: "Get up, take the child and his mother and run away to Egypt, and stay there until I tell you to leave. Herod will be looking for the child to kill him." [14] So Joseph got up, took the child and his mother, and left during the night for Egypt, [15] where he stayed until Herod died.

This was done to make come true what the Lord had said through the prophet, "I called my Son out of Egypt."

The disappearance of the astrologers made Herod nervous. He who did not hesitate to kill his own children would stop at nothing to destroy a rival king. Again it is impressive that Joseph acts upon his dream. Many people have experiences of precognition but not all act on it. But Joseph by now had learned to trust his dreams. When the angel came in the dream, Joseph did not even wait until morning. He arose, and left for Egypt.

The histories of Israel and Egypt have been intertwined over centuries. In the last decade the two nations have fought a number of times. They have not always been enemies. Early in biblical history, Abraham traveled to Egypt. Many Jews came to live in Egypt as a result of drought conditions and Joseph's preferment in the Pharaoh's house. One of Israel's greatest leaders, Moses, was educated in a prince's household in Egypt. It was not inappropriate, therefore, when exile for Joseph and Mary was necessary that it be in Egypt.

The length of this sojourn in Egypt is not known. Mary and Joseph could well have known people there. A million Jews lived in the city of Alexandria, Egypt, on the coast. The Coptic Church of Mary the Virgin claims that it is built over the spot where the holy family lived. The death of Herod the Great brought this exile to a close.

The prophecy referred to is Hosea 11:1, a clear reference to God's leading of Israel out of Egypt. In the light of what happened in Jesus Christ, early Christians who searched the Scriptures understood the passage to point forward. This type of individual word or partial sentence interpretation of Scripture is strange to the modern ear. But it was common enough in the early church.

2:16

[16] When Herod realized that the visitors from the east had tricked him, he was furious. He gave orders to kill all the boys in Bethlehem and its neighborhood who were two years old and younger — in accordance with what he had learned from the visitors about the time when the star had appeared.

The massacre of the Holy Innocents is one of the more dastardly crimes of the ancient world. Herod would clearly stop at nothing to preserve his throne. The sinner in us takes some delight in the manner of his own death — slow, tortured, bloated, racked by worms and filled with delusions. A comparable act of violence was perpetrated by the Pharaoh in the time of Moses. Moses, too, survived, raised in the court of Pharaoh. The enemy raised right in the bosom, so to speak. And the crime of the Pharaoh is also visited upon him in the terrible Passover described in Exodus 12, where the first born of Egypt are struck down by the angel of death.

Herod's brutality was without success. Like Hitler's murder of millions of Jews, the desired result was not attained. Hitler died a pathetic suicide in a Berlin bunker. The blood of Jewish martyrs was the seed of a new nation of Israel. Herod failed to snuff out the life which was also to become the seed of a new Israel.

2:17, 18

[17] In this way what the prophet Jeremiah had said came true:
[18] "A sound is heard in Ramah,
The sound of bitter crying and weeping.
Rachel weeps for her children,
She weeps and will not be comforted,
Because they are all dead."

The quotation is from Jeremiah 31:15. Matthew does not say this happened in order to fulfill the Scripture, as he often says, but "in this way what the prophet

Jeremiah had said came true." There is an important distinction here. God is not the agent of evil in the world. It was not his wish that innocent children should die. That was the act of a paranoid king who wished to live forever.

Anyone who has lost a child knows the inconsolable nature of such grief. Possibilities for a fresh life cut off. Motherhood dedicated to a new generation unfulfilled. No funeral is so sad as that of a child. And words of comfort are difficult to find.

In Jeremiah itself words of comfort do follow this passage. The people of Israel would return from exile. There would be fulfillment. God sees farther than humans see.

But the grief of children lost would not be cut off.

2:19-21

[19] After Herod had died, an angel of the Lord appeared in a dream to Joseph, in Egypt, and said: [20] "Get up, take the child and his mother, and go back to the country of Israel. Because those who tried to kill the child are dead." [21] So Joseph got up, took the child and his mother, and went back to the country of Israel.

Herod the Great died in what is now called the year four before Christ. How, one might ask, could the King under whom Jesus was born have died before he was born? The answer is not the fault of Scriptures, but of later calendar makers and their calculations. The letters A.D., such as A.D. 1945, stand for the Latin ANNO DOMINI, "in the year of our Lord." This designation was developed by the monk, Dionysius Exiguus in the year 532. He began his system with the date he thought was the year of Jesus' birth. Today it is known that he was a few years off. The designation B.C. began later to designate those years before Christ. Prior to this, the system of dating was related to the current ruler, as illustrated in Luke 3:1, 2.

Herod's death cleared the way for Joseph's return to his native land. Again the way he learned of it was through a dream. And again he acted on the basis of what he learned.

2:22, 23

[22] When he heard that Archelaus had succeeded his father Herod as king of Judea, Joseph was afraid to settle there. He was given more instructions in a dream, and so went to the province of Galilee [23] and made his home in a town called Nazareth. He did this to make come true what the prophets had said, "He will be called a Nazarene."

Herod's kingdom was divided among three sons. Even though he had killed many of his children, at least three survived him. The eldest of these, Archelaus, received Judea (in which were Jerusalem and Bethlehem) Samaria and Idumaea (from which territory Herod's family originally came). Archelaus also received the title king. Herod's son Antipas received Galilee and Peraea and the title Tetrarch. His son Philip, also Tetrarch, received Gaulonitis, Trachonitis, and Paneas.

Joseph did not rely only upon dreams for his decisions. When he learned that Archelaus had been given control of Judea, he feared to settle there. His fears were well founded. Archelaus soon showed himself to be a bloody ruler, too bloody even for the Romans. He was exiled to Gaul and a Roman was sent to rule in his stead with the area declared a military province. It was to this rule that Pilate would come in the year A.D. 25.

On the basis of further dreams, Joseph eventually settled in Galilee, in a little town called Nazareth which lies between the Mediterranean and the Sea of Galilee. This province, ruled by Herod Antipas, had only been Jewish for about 100 years. Most residents were Gentile still. Some Gentiles had been forcibly converted to Judaism. The only families which were old Jewish families had, like Joseph's, migrated from the south.

The move to the North meant that Jesus would survive to adulthood. A youthful observer of the biblical story, in noting that Jesus escaped the massacre of the innocents, was pleased that they didn't get Jesus until later. It meant that he lived in a less intense environment for the early part of his life. He would get to know Jerusalem soon enough.

The prophecy referred to by Matthew in verse 23 is not known.

Matthew 3

Matthew 3:1-3

[1] At that time John the Baptist came and started preaching in the desert of Judea. [2] "Change your ways," he said, "for the Kingdom of heaven is near!" [3] John was the one that the prophet Isaiah was talking about when he said:
"Someone is shouting in the desert:
'Get the Lord's road ready for him,
Make a straight path for him to travel!'"

The Gospel of Matthew shifts from the early youth of Jesus in Galilee of the north, to the preaching of his cousin, nicknamed "the Baptizer," some twenty-five years later.

John's message is one of repentance. He called upon people to change their way of living, because the Kingdom of heaven is at hand. This initial preaching of the kingdom of heaven is the central proclamation of the ministry of Jesus. Kingdom of God or Kingdom of heaven (or heavens) refers to that area or domain in which the power of God holds sway. "Has drawn near" can mean with reference to time or space.

Participation or involvement in this kingdom requires an abandonment of previous investments and commitments.

Matthew understands John in the light of a passage from Isaiah 40:3. The prophecy at its first level no doubt referred to the return of the Jews from Babylonian exile. It speaks of a construction of a super highway over miles of desert and mountain. When Matthew reads the passage, he sees it as a passage identifying John. In his reading the desert does not refer to the area through which the road is built, but the area in which the prophecy is made.

In the intention of God, the prophecy was probably intended for both occasions.

3:4-6

[4] John's clothes were made of camel's hair; he wore a leather belt around his waist, and ate locusts and wild honey. [5] People came to him

*from Jerusalem, from the whole province of Judea, and from all the
country around the Jordan river. [6] They confessed their sins and he
baptized them in the Jordan.*

John is a rough character. He wore neither wool nor
linen but camel's hair. He did not eat domestic food, but
lived off the land by catching grasshoppers and raiding
wild bee hives.

His preaching awakened the hunger of hearts for
God. People flocked to him from the city and the
surrounding regions. John baptized those who confessed
their sins as a token of their readiness to participate in
the Kingdom of heaven.

The baptism practiced by John should not be judged
by later Christian baptism, but should be judged by the
act itself. It was administered to adults, apparently, who
wished to be ready to participate in the Kingdom. It
required their coming forward and John's baptism. And
it took place in the Jordan River.

3:7-12

*[7] When John saw many Pharisees and Sadducees coming to him to
be baptized, he said the them; "You snakes — who told you that you
could escape from God's wrath that is about to come? [8] Do the things
that will show that you have changed your ways. [9] And do not think
you can excuse yourselves by saying, 'Abraham is our father.' I tell you
that God can take these rocks and make children for Abraham! [10] The
ax is ready to cut the trees at the roots; every tree that does not bear
good fruit will be cut down and thrown in the fire. [11] I baptize you with
water to show that you have repented; but the one who will come after
me will baptize you with the Holy Spirit and fire. He is much greater
than I am; I am not good enough even to carry his sandals. [12] He has
his winnowing-shovel with him to thresh out all the grain; he will gather
his wheat into his barn, but burn the chaff in a fire that never goes out!"*

This section is a summary of John's preaching. It
addresses itself to Pharisees and Sadducees, two
respectable leadership groups within Judaism. The
identical section in Luke (3:7-9) is not addressed to
Pharisees and Sadducees in particular but to all the
crowds coming out. Matthew perhaps added the names
of the two groups to specify that it was religious people
who came out and not simply people who did not practice
their religion.

John's severity is indicated by his address: "offspring of vipers." "Who warned you to flee from the coming wrath?" In his first line is indicated his belief that the kingdom's coming would be a coming of violence. Further he made it clear that simple verbal repentance without changed lives would be useless. Appeals to length of family tenure in Judaism were viewed as of no avail. God could raise up descendants of Abraham from the plentiful stones of the Judaean landscape.

Verse 10 reinforces the notion that the coming Kingdom is both near and severe. Language of cutting down, harvest, fire — all this points to the finality of the events unfolding. Yet John is preparing. He baptized with water. But one to come would baptize with the **Holy Spirit** and with **fire**.

The Holy Spirit is clear enough. The pouring out of the Spirit was experienced at Pentecost. Jesus made that possible. But the fire is not so easy to interpret. Perhaps it pointed in part to the travail which was soon to come on Jerusalem. The double message is there in Acts too (2:17-21), both spirit and fire.

John did not consider himself a rival to Jesus, but a forerunner of a judge. The one who followed would bring the harvest.

3:13-17

[13] *At that time Jesus went from Galilee to the Jordan, and came to John to be baptized by him.* [14] *But John tried to make him change his mind. "I ought to be baptized by you," John said, "yet you come to me!"* [15] *But Jesus answered him, "Let it be this way for now. For in this way we shall do all that God requires." So John agreed.*
[16] *As soon as Jesus was baptized, he came up out of the water. Then heaven was opened to him, and he saw the Spirit of God coming down like a dove and lighting on him.* [17] *And then a voice said from heaven, "This is my own dear Son, with whom I am well pleased."*

The Jordan River runs from Galilee down to Judea and empties into the Dead Sea. Somewhere on that route, Jesus came out to be baptized by John. John recognized Jesus as his superior. The reader is not told how. When John hesitated to baptize Jesus, Jesus insisted. Again the reader is not told why. Except that God requires it. Perhaps this points to Jesus' own sense that he must walk in life as a man, obedient to God's law and subordinate to God's will in every way. In this way he would fulfill all righteousness.

The most important thing that happened to Jesus in his baptism was that he received the gift of the Holy Spirit. In this period prior to Pentecost, the Spirit came only especially upon certain individuals. This represented a vocation on the part of that person to do the will of God at the same time as it was an empowering to do it.

The most spectacular thing that happened at the baptism of Jesus was the heavenly voice. God did not leave doubt about Jesus' origin or identity, but claims him as beloved son, with whom he is pleased.

30

Matthew 4

Matthew 4:1-4

[1] Then the Spirit led Jesus into the desert to be tempted by the Devil. [2] After spending forty days and nights without food, Jesus was hungry. [3] The Devil came to him and said, "If you are God's Son, order these stones to turn into bread." [4] Jesus answered, "The scripture says, 'Man cannot live on bread alone, but on every word that God speaks.'"

The first place the Holy Spirit led Jesus was to the devil. That certainly seems like a contradiction. In the very prayer Jesus taught Christians to pray he says, "Lead us not into temptation." Yet here that is exactly what God did. Like the story of Job. God knows that Satan will contend mightily for a righteous man. Rather than postpone that battle, God apparently thought it ought to be fought right away. There is also perhaps an element here of a necessary testing to be sure of the vocational resolve. Jesus was later to say, "He that puts his hand to the plow and then looks back is not worthy of me."

The first temptation was to satisfy a physical need. After forty days hunger would be a consuming drive. In the Devil's taunt, there is also a question of Jesus' identity. "If you are the son of God" — if you are divine, prove it by making these stones into bread.

Jesus' response to Satan, drawn from Deuteronomy 8:3, is particularly impressive because it is quoted by a man who has not eaten for forty days. It is a passage that can be misused if it is used to turn aside the legitimate claims for help of the poor or dependent. But it is a profound truth to a materialistic society. Meaning does not lie in the abundance of worldly goods, but in the hearing and obeying of the word of God.

4:5-7

[5] Then the Devil took Jesus to the Holy City, set him on the highest point of the Temple, [6] and said to him, "If you are God's Son, throw yourself down to the ground; for the scripture says,
'God will give orders to his angels about you:

They will hold you up with their hands,
So that you will not even hurt your feet on the stones.'"
[7] *Jesus answered, "But the scripture also says, 'You must not put the Lord your God to the test.'"*

The second temptation is the temptation to test God's devotion and is a challenge to Jesus' faith. The passage Satan quotes is Psalms 91:11-12. In the Psalms it refers to any who call upon the name of the Lord. If Jesus were to jump off the temple wall, he would prove his confidence in God. But by doing so he would be testing God, requiring him to be faithful to his promise.

Such a faith would place greater emphasis upon one's own certainty and confidence than it would on the object of that faith, God. Thus, it is that Jesus quoted Deuteronomy 6:16 in response.

Many commentators on this passage have noted that Satan tempts Jesus through the use of Scripture. There are at least two lessons in this. First, Satan is no dummy. He is profoundly intelligent, and can use any good within the created order which will aid him in getting the creatures to put themselves before the Creator. That was his sin, which he still will not admit is sin. Therefore, the more souls he can involve in this rebellion, the more satisfied he feels.

A second lesson in Satan's use of the Bible is the simple fact that the Bible can be misused. It has been used by the unscrupulous to justify slavery, slave wages, and for a host of other abuses. The use of the Bible without the spirit of God is no guarantor of truth.

4:8-11

[8] *Then the Devil took Jesus to a very high mountain and showed him all the kingdoms of the world, in all their greatness. [9] "All this I will give you," the Devil said, "If you kneel down and worship me." [10] Then Jesus answered, "Go away, Satan! The scripture says, 'Worship the Lord your God and serve only him!'"*
[11] *So the Devil left him; and the angels came and helped Jesus.*

From what earthly mountain can one see all of the kingdoms of the world? There is none. This probably means that this trip was taken in a vision. Jesus never traveled physically outside of the Holy Land in his adult life. But here he had a chance to see Rome, Athens, Antioch, Babylon, and other great cities. Therefore when the Devil offered him "all this," he had a good idea what he was refusing.

One wonders whether the Devil was bluffing a little bit at this point. Could he actually have delivered such earthly power? Of course if Jesus had thrown in his lot with Satan, they would have made a formidable team. Later when Jesus marched into Jerusalem he had a crowd willing to make him king.

And the price for such wealth and power? Only the worship of the Devil. That which Satan would not freely give to God he desperately wanted from God's Son.

Jesus' answer comes from Deuteronomy 6:13. Again he places himself within the protection of the Bible, which proved a solid resource for him throughout the temptations.

At the conclusion of the temptations, the angels came to minister to him. He had to experience the Devil's onslaught with no special revelation or support. Only the will of God as he knew it from the Bible was his support. What he had and what was sufficient to triumph over every temptation, is available to every Christian.

4:12-17

[12] *When Jesus heard that John had been put in prison, he went away to Galilee.* [13] *He did not settle down in Nazareth, but went and lived in Capernaum, a town by Lake Galilee, in the territory of Zebulun and Naphtali.* [14] *This was done to make come true what the prophet Isaiah had said:*

[15] *"Land of Zebulun, land of Naphtali,*
In the direction of the sea, on the other side of Jordan,
Galilee of the Gentiles!
[16] *The people who live in darkness*
Will see a great light!
On those who live in the dark land of death
The light will shine!"

[17] *From that time Jesus began to preach his message: "Turn away from your sins! The Kingdom of heaven is near!"*

John's imprisonment was the signal for Jesus to begin his ministry. He returned to Galilee, but not to the town in which he was raised. Instead he located on the north end of the Sea of Galilee in the town of Capernaum. In this city today can be seen Peter's house. Still standing also is a synagogue built only 100 years after Jesus, likely on the foundations of the synagogue of Jesus' time.

In Isaiah 9:1-2, Matthew has found a good prophecy to attach to the fact that Jesus carried out the early part of his ministry from Capernaum.

The message which Jesus preached is said in summary to be identical to that of John. "Repent, for the Kingdom of heaven has drawn near."

4:18-22

[18] *As Jesus walked by Lake Galilee, he saw two brothers who were fishermen, Simon [called Peter] and his brother Andrew, catching fish in the lake with a net. [19] Jesus said to them, "Come with me and I will teach you to catch men." [20] At once they left their nets and went with him.*

[21] *He went on and saw two other brothers, James and John, the sons of Zebedee. They were in their boat with their father Zebedee, getting their nets ready. Jesus called them; [22] at once they left the boat and their father, and went with Jesus.*

A walk by the Sea of Galilee would have been only two hundred yards from Jesus' house in Capernaum. The lake was the center of a small fishing industry. Simon Peter and Andrew were the first disciples selected for a new enterprise, the catching of people. The rapidity with which they decided and left their nets is breathtaking. The Gospel of John reports (1:35-42) that Andrew had first been a disciple of John and had come to Jesus through John. Andrew then led his brother Peter to Jesus. At any rate, whatever the exact process, the first two disciples selected were handworkers like Jesus himself.

A second set of brothers, James and John, were recruited at the same time. They left their father (according to Mark 1:20, with the hired helpers) and joined Jesus.

The rapidity with which these disciples chose to follow Jesus is an object lesson in life. The good things, the big things, the right things happen fast and the opportunity is fleeting. Others were offered the opportunity to follow Jesus and hesitated. In each instance the offer was withdrawn or Jesus simply moved on. God is involved in the accomplishment of his purposes. People are offered the chance to be a part. But the offer does not stand open forever. God is able to raise up sons of Abraham from stones, if he must.

4:23-25

[23] *Jesus went all over Galilee, teaching in their meeting houses, preaching the Good News of the Kingdom, and healing people from every kind of disease and sickness.* [24] *The news about him spread through the whole country of Syria, so that people brought him all those who were sick with all kinds of diseases, and afflicted with all sorts of troubles: people with demons, and epileptics and paralytics — Jesus healed them all.* [25] *Great crowds followed him from Galilee and the Ten Towns, from Jerusalem, Judea, and the land on the other side of the Jordan.*

Jesus went out on his mission. It was a mission of preaching and healing. This twofold division still characterizes the church's efforts: (1) The proclamation of the gospel and (2) the restoration to health.

His impact was not limited to Jews. Much of Galilee was Gentile as was all of the region of the ten towns to the east of the Jordan. He was sought out as a healer. When he preached he went first to the synagogues, lay Jewish centers where any male Jew was permitted to speak. Paul would later follow the same strategy.

Matthew 5

Matthew 5:1-6

[1] Jesus saw the crowds and went up a hill, where he sat down. His disciples gathered around him, [2] and he began to teach them:
[3] "Happy are those who know they are spiritually poor;
the Kingdom of heaven belongs to them!
[4] "Happy are those who mourn:
God will comfort them!
[5] "Happy are the meek:
they will receive what God has promised!
[6] "Happy are those whose greatest desire is to do what God
requires:
God will satisfy them fully!"

The next three chapters represent a collection of Jesus' teaching. It is presented as having been given all at one time and in one place, as well it might have.

The sermon begins with nine blessings, or beatitudes. A number of them are also found in Luke 6:20-22.

The sermon is addressed the the "have nots" of society. While parts of Judaism, just as parts of contemporary Christianity, saw material abundance as a sign of God's favor, Jesus clearly saw as the focus of his mission those who had nothing of the world's goods or religious position but who desired a right relationship to God.

The opposite of the poor in spirit in verse three are the proud. Luke simply identifies them as the poor. But it is the humble who can be open to the action of God. The proud cannot open themselves to it. A good example of this has been the response of Christian denominations to the Charismatic movement. The proud say, "God has done everything he will do and has committed it to us." But others look and say perhaps God is doing something new in our midst.

"Blessed are those who mourn." The person who has not suffered has missed much that life has to offer. Not least the consolation which God can give!

"Blessed are the meek because they shall inherit the earth" is an additional promise that in God's world the race does not go to the swift and powerful. The millionaires of the world shall not inherit it. True, they hold its goods for a time. But the true heirs are the meek.

"Those who hunger and thirst for righteousness — will be satisfied." People who look at world events and ask why the wicked prosper and the righteous suffer, will have their answer. The apparent injustices of this world will be corrected. Right will prevail and prosper.

5:7-12

[7] *"Happy are those who show mercy to others:*
God will show mercy to them!
[8] *"Happy are the pure in heart:*
they will see God!
[9] *"Happy are those who work for peace among men:*
God will call them his sons!
[10] *"Happy are those who suffer persecution because they do what*
God requires:
the Kingdom of heaven belongs to them!
[11] *"Happy are you when men insult you and mistreat you and tell all*
kinds of evil lies against you because you are my followers. [12] *Rejoice*
and be glad, because a great reward is kept for you in heaven. This is
how men mistreated the prophets who lived before you."

God will be merciful to those who show mercy. The theme returns in many places, not least in the prayer which Jesus himself taught. "Forgive us our trespasses (debts) as we forgive those who trespass against us." Human conduct sets the pattern for divine orientation. To many that is not a comforting message. But it is a description of the kingdom.

Those with clean hearts will be ushered into God's presence. God has no truck with the sneer, the snide condescension that looks with jaundiced eye upon the world. Cleanliness of heart includes an intimate capacity to be fooled rather than the worldly wisdom of the one who could not recognize righteousness if it hit him in the face.

"Blessed are the peacemakers." Those who say the business of the church is limited to preaching will be unhappy with this passage. How difficult to make peace and how easy to unleash the dogs of war, whether of nations or in simple human communities. Dag Hammarskjold was a peacemaker in his years as Secretary General of the United Nations. It came as genuine surprise to people when a diary was discovered among his effects which revealed a deep devotion to Jesus Christ. Here was a famous man who lived out this beatitude as his particular vocation. But the same vocation is lived out in families, business, and industry.

"Blessed are those who are persecuted for the sake of righteousness." The popular song, "I beg your pardon, I never promised you a rose garden" catches a fundamental truth about Christianity. A religion built around a leader who ended his this-worldly sojourn on a cross should not expect a plush and easy life. But it is those who suffer on behalf of righteousness to whom the Kingdom belongs!

Persecution for Christ's sake means great reward in heaven. It is to be placed in the company of the prophets.

Of course everyone of these beatitudes will not be represented by every person. As a model for human conduct they could lead people to despair, but as a model of what God values, no better charter of his Kingdom could be revealed.

5:13-16

[13] "You are like salt for the earth. If the salt loses its taste, there is no way to make it salty again. It has become worthless, and so it is thrown away where people walk on it.

[14] "You are like the light for the world. A city built on a high hill cannot be hid. [15] Nobody lights a lamp to put it under a bowl; instead he puts it on the lamp-stand, where it gives light for everyone in the house. [16] In the same way your light must shine before people, so that they will see the good things you do and give praise to your Father in heaven."

The glory and the potential of Christianity is revealed in the salt saying as well as its potential for falling short. To be the salt of the earth is indeed a high calling. Christians give it flavor, enhance all the natural qualities that are there in the creation. But if Christians should fail, it is they and not the earth that are to be judged worthy only to be trodden under foot. With opportunity comes the possibility of failure. If God can raise up sons of Abraham from stones, neither is he bound by the performance of Christians.

Christianity is a vocation. It is not a condition. To be a light is nothing unless it is a light for someone or something. A radiant life attracts attention and brings glory to God, where it belongs.

5:17-19a

[17] *"Do not think that I have come to do away with the Law of Moses and the teaching of the prophets. I have not come to do away with them, but to give them real meaning. [18] Remember this! As long as heaven and earth last, the least point or the smallest detail of the Law will not be done away with — not until the end of all things. [19a] Therefore, whoever breaks even the smallest of the commandments, and teaches others to do the same, will be least in the Kingdom of heaven.*

This section begins Matthew's most characteristic emphasis: The sharpening of the Law. Jesus' positive affirmation of the Law here is repeated in no other Gospel. In fact, there is tension between a strong support of the Law here and the attitude of Paul.

Certainly Jesus intended to fulfill the intent of the Law, the provision of an equitable and God-fearing society; such a society would be by definition the Kingdom of God. Still it is difficult to imagine Jesus affirming the entire Law. (The written Law includes the first five books of the Bible. The oral Law included the teachings of the Pharisees, later written up as the Mishnah.) A good exercise for anyone is simply to read through Leviticus to realize how far modern Christians are from observing the whole Law.

5:19b, 20

[19b] *On the other hand, whoever obeys the Law, and teaches others to do the same, will be great in the Kingdom of heaven. [20] I tell you, then, you will be able to enter the Kingdom of heaven only if your standard of life is far above the standard of the teachers of the Law and the Pharisees."*

This section reveals that for the community of Matthew the chief competition was the Pharisees. They had established the mark to shoot for. But one would have to do better than they did.

5:21-26

[21] *"You have heard that men were told in the past, 'Do not murder; anyone who commits murder will be brought before the judge.' [22] But now I tell you: whoever is angry with his brother will be brought before the judge; whoever calls his brother 'You good-for-nothing!' will be brought before the Council; and whoever calls his brother a worthless fool will be in danger of going to the fire of hell. [23] So if you are about to offer your gift to God at the altar and there you remember that your brother has something against you, [24] leave your gift there in front of the altar and go at once to make peace with your brother; then come back and offer your gift to God.*

[25] "If a man brings a lawsuit against you and takes you to court, be friendly with him while there is time, before you get to court; once you are there he will turn you over to the judge, who will hand you over to the police, and you will be put in jail. [26] There you will stay, I tell you, until you pay the last penny of your fine."

Jesus here establishes rules for the Kingdom. They are more severe than the Law of Moses. Anger is now as serious as murder once was. The belittling of one's fellow human is enough to make one liable to hell. Fractured relationships interfere in one's liturgical celebration.

The parable of the lawsuit suggests that the only place where one can get a lenient hearing is by working toward an out-of-court settlement with the aggrieved party. Once one becomes involved in the regular legal process, there is nothing but a severe future. This story is consistent with the theme sounded earlier about the opportunity but also the expendibility of people in the light of the great work God is doing.

5:27-30

[27] *"You have heard that it was said, 'Do not commit adultery.' [28] But now I tell you: anyone who looks at a woman and wants to possess her is guilty of committing adultery with her in his heart. [29] So if your right eye causes you to sin, take it out and throw it away! It is much better for you to lose a part of your body than to have your whole body thrown into hell. [30] If your right hand causes you to sin, cut it off and throw it away! It is much better for you to lose one of your limbs than to have your whole body go off to hell."*

The saying on adultery represents the clearest

example of the internalization of the Law. As long as the Law was viewed as a regulator of human conduct, it was theoretically possible to fulfill. But when Law is extended to cover also secret thoughts, it is no longer possible to fulfill. Unlikely the only adult male who has never looked at a woman and wanted to possess her is a homosexual. And he has troubles of another kind.

But the answer of this passage asks for radical surgery. Pluck out the eye! Cut off the hand! Jesus likely meant these as metaphors. But the stakes are intensely serious. "Better for you to lose one of your limbs than to have your whole body go off to hell."

5:31, 32

[31] "It was also said, 'Anyone who divorces his wife must give her a written notice of divorce.' [32] But now I tell you: if a man divorces his wife, and she has not been unfaithful, then he is guilty of making her commmit adultery if she marries again; and the man who marries her also commits adultery."

Jesus also set a radically higher standard for marriage. In Judaism a woman was considered next to property. She could be returned to her father more easily than she had been obtained from him.

What Jesus did in his elevation of marriage was to place woman on an equal footing with a man. This was consistent with his desire to reveal in this sermon God's intention for humanity.

5:33-37

[33] "You have also heard that men were told in the past, 'Do not break your promise, but do what you have sworn to do before the Lord.' [34] But now I tell you: do not use any vow when you make a promise; do not swear by heaven, because it is God's throne; [35] nor by earth, because it is the resting place for his feet; nor by Jerusalem, because it is the city of the great King. [36] Do not even swear by your head, because you cannot make a single hair white or black. [37] Just say 'Yes' or 'No' — anything else you have to say comes from the Evil One."

This is one of the harder sayings of Jesus. It emphasizes the absolute integrity expected from humanity on the one side and the sacredness of all of God's creation on the other.

When Jesus says that anything additional to yes and no is of the evil one, it is a recognition of Satan's title as father of lies. The introduction of an oath invokes the name of God in some matter of controversy. Such an introduction can be used by Satan.

Ordinary cursing and swearing is not under discussion specifically in this passage. Of course Jesus would have no use for it.

5:38-42

[38] "You have heard that it was said, 'An eye for an eye, and a tooth for a tooth.' [39] But now I tell you: do not take revenge on someone who does you wrong. If anyone slaps you on the right cheek, let him slap your left cheek too. [40] And if someone takes you to court to sue you for your shirt, let him have your coat as well. [41] And if one of the occupation troops forces you to carry his pack one mile, carry it another mile. [42] When someone asks you for something, give it to him; when someone wants to borrow something, lend it to him."

The law of retribution in its introduction was a fair law. It set a limit to what kind of vengeance could be extracted for a crime. It put an effective end to blood feuds.

But here again Jesus moves far beyond a concept of justice to a policy of cooperation with aggressors and oppressors. Christians are both attracted and frightened by such counsel. Is it really possible to cooperate in such a way with people who would take advantage of others? Is it right to do so? What if one is responsible for the protection of others?

Many questions emerge. But the position taken by Jesus is not vague or complicated. He urges that self-giving generosity rather than even-handed justice characterize the Christian's relations with others.

5:43-48

[43] "You have heard that it was said, 'Love your friends, hate your enemies.' [44] But now I tell you: love your enemies, and pray for those who mistreat you, [45] so that you will become the sons of your Father in heaven. For he makes his sun to shine on bad and good people alike, and gives rain to those who do right and those who do wrong. [46] Why should you expect God to reward you, if you love only the people who

42

love you? Even the tax collectors do that! [47] And if you speak only to your friends, have you done anything out of the ordinary? Even the pagans do that! [48] You must be perfect — just as your Father in heaven is perfect."

The model of conduct is clearly that of God himself. Loving friends and hating enemies is belittled as the conduct of natural man, of tax collectors (a not-admired segment of Jewish society) and Gentiles. But those who wish to become children of God ought to act like God. And to act like God is to love the unlovely, to speak to the rejected, to love enemies.

Nothing less than the perfection of God is held out as a model to strive for.

Matthew 6

Matthew 6:1-4

[1] "Be careful not to perform your religious duties in public so that people will see what you do. If you do these things publicly you will not have any reward from your Father in heaven.

[2] "So when you give something to a needy person, do not make a big show of it, as the show-offs do in the meeting houses and on the streets. They do it so that people will praise them. Remember this! They have already been paid in full. [3] But when you help a needy person, do it in such a way that even your closest friend will not know about it, [4] but it will be a private matter. And your Father, who sees what you do in private, will reward you."

The context of this passage is the question of reward for religious and ethical actions. Public acts will of necessity gain public approval. If one has public approval, then no further approval is possible. To insure that approval be granted by God for good acts, they must be done quietly and secretly. .

6:5-8

[5] "And when you pray, do not be like the show-offs! They love to stand up and pray in the meeting houses and on the street corners so that everybody will see them. Remember this! They have already been paid in full. [6] But when you pray, go to your room and close the door, and pray to your Father who is unseen. And your Father, who sees what you do in private, will reward you.

[7] "In your prayers do not use a lot of words, as the pagans do, who think that God will hear them because of their long prayers. [8] Do not be like them; God is your Father and he already knows what you need before you ask him."

Being natural can be one of the most difficult things in the world. What is so easy for children becomes lost in adults, who learn to worry about what other people will think or who seek to impress others. Jesus in this teaching reminds Christians that prayer is to be addressed to God.

He offered specific advice. Go into your room to remind yourself what the prayer is for and to whom it is addressed.

Jesus also commends simplicity. No big words, just a simple expression from the heart since God already knows the need.

44

6:9-13

[9] *This is the way you should pray:*
    'Our Father in heaven:
    May your name be kept holy,
[10] *May your Kingdom come,*
    May your will be done on earth as it is in heaven.
[11] *Give us today the food we need;*
[12] *Forgive us what we owe you as we forgive what others owe us;*
[13] *Do not bring us to hard testing, but keep us safe from the Evil One.'*

How relevant Jesus is 2,000 years later is clearly indicated by the prayer he taught.

First he honors God. Then he seeks his kingdom. Then he seeks his will. These first petitions are a part of one piece. They focus on God and what his purposes are. When this is kept in focus, other things fall into place. Jesus lived this order of things in his own ministry.

Second, he recognizes people's needs. Those needs are for **food, forgiveness,** and **future.** Every man and woman needs his and her share of the world's goods. Many problems of this world grow out of an unequal or inadequate distribution of wealth. Here it is that socialism and communism have a genuine appeal when they focus on a fairer distribution of money and property.

Forgiveness makes life possible. Humans have the gift of speech, the power to lash out in a cutting way at others. But when one person has succeeded in cutting off another, only forgiveness can restore that relationship. This prayer prays for that measure of forgiveness which the person who prays has been willing to extend to others.

The future is for keeps for humans. The human race is fragile; the hold of each person on sanity, health, love, companionship is subject to disruption. No one can be confident of his or her ability to stand whatever blows life may bring. This prayer is a frank admission of weakness. Do not allow us to come into temptation. Stand between us and Satan. Luther, when beset by the Devil, reminded him that he was a baptized Christian. That is a formula which still provides protection today.

6:14, 15

[14] "For if you forgive others the wrongs they have done you, your Father in heaven will forgive you. [15] But if you do not forgive others, then your Father in heaven will not forgive the wrongs you have done."

This theme is repeated in bare simplicity at many points in the Gospels. In the life of each person the power is given to determine whether or not he will receive forgiveness at the hand of God. This is not a requirement for holiness, but for generosity. It seems to ask little. But people who have been wronged find forgiveness one of the most difficult acts there is.

6:16-18

[16] "And when you fast, do not put on a sad face like the show-offs do. They go around with a hungry look so that everybody will be sure to see that they are fasting. Remember this! They have already been paid in full. [17] When you go without food, wash your face and comb your hair, [18] so that others cannot know that you are fasting — only your Father, who is unseen, will know. And your Father, who sees what you do in private, will reward you."

Perhaps the most important word in this saying is the first "when." "When you fast, " says Jesus, not "if you fast." He assumed a continuation of the ancient religious practice of fasting.

What is a fast? It is the practice of refraining from eating food (and in some cases drink) for periods of time from a few hours and up. It has had a variety of meanings through history. It can be a sign of mind over body. It can be a sign of repentance, as it apparently is in this passage. It can be for the purpose of attuning oneself to the realm of the Spirit, as it seems to have been when Jesus went out into the wilderness prior to the beginning of his ministry.

Jesus did not question the value of a fast. He affirmed it by his own practice. What he says here is that it ought not to be done to impress others. Only if it is done in relation to God and not people will it be rewarded by God. For it is only God who sees the soul. A few decades ago, Oscar Wilde's story, **The Portrait of Dorian Grey,** revealed how a young man sold his soul to the devil in exchange for eternal youth. Only Mr. Grey's portrait, which he eventually hid in his attic, revealed the corruption of his soul. But his face continued virtuous and unlined. Many people succeed in hiding their souls from their fellow human beings. But God, who searches the secrets of people's hearts, is not deceived. He knows both the act and the motivation.

6:19-21

[19] *"Do not save riches here on earth, where rust and worms destroy, and robbers break in and steal. [20] Instead, save riches in heaven, where rust and worms cannot destroy, and robbers cannot break in and steal. [21] For your heart will always be where your riches are."*

Jesus was not impressed by accumulated wealth. He enjoyed the things money can buy. He lived well in the homes of the wealthy. He appreciated the costly ointment which was used to anoint him. But he also knew wealth was little to count on for two reasons.

Wealth can be stolen. It is the rich who have elaborate burglar alarm systems, guards at the gate, body guards, guns, elaborate locks. And every precaution yet devised by humans can be eluded by humans. Many rich live in a constant state of unease about their possessions.

"Where your treasure is, there is your heart" points to the overinvestment people make in the goods of the world. The person so overlyinvested has neither the time nor the heart to lay up treasures in heaven.

Of course, many rich people (and most North Americans are rich by a global standard) use great portions of their wealth to lay up treasures in heaven. But the thrust of this saying of Jesus is that people with big bank accounts are not able to take it with them. The treasures that people can enjoy in heaven are fruits of love and acts of kindness.

6:22, 23

[22] *"The eyes are like a lamp for the body: if your eyes are clear,*

your whole body will be full of light; [23] *but if your eyes are bad, your body will be in darkness. So if the light in you is darkness, how terribly dark it will be!"*

This saying is difficult to understand in this translation. The key word is **haplous,** translated here as clear. The word can also be translated single, in the sense of singleness of purpose. If a person's eye is pure (unmixed) then it will be like a breath of fresh air or bright light to the body. The contrasting situation is one in which the eye is corrupt [**Poneros**]. Then everything that enters the body through the vision is corrupted.

There are proverbs in English that bear witness to the same truth. "Beauty is in the eye of the beholder." "To the pure all things are pure."

A graphic illustration of this parable is present in modern medicine, where heavy smokers and people who live in polluted areas have been found to have almost black lungs, a result of these white sponges having been daily treated to doses of unclean air.

The moral of the story is never to lose a capacity for putting the most charitable construction on human activity. Do not look on the world with jaundiced eye, but with a "single" eye.

6:24-27

[24] *"No one can be a slave to two masters: he will hate one and love the other; he will be loyal to one and despise the other. So it is with you: you cannot have both God and wealth as your master.*

[25] *"This is why I tell you: do not be worried about the food and drink you need to stay alive, or about clothes for your body. After all, isn't life worth more than food? and isn't the body worth more than clothes?* [26] *Look at the birds flying around: they do not plant seeds, gather a harvest, and put it in barns; your Father in heaven takes care of them! Aren't you worth much more than birds?* [27] *Which one of you can live a few years more by worrying about it?"*

The saying about two masters is appropriate. In modern times one could add the notion that many people have that they serve no master at all, but are completely independent. With political independence in the great democracies of the world has often come the notion of the self-reliant person. The idea of the self-made man is still very much alive in modern society.

But the Bible recognizes no independent people. Everyone will serve a master. It may not be in slavery. Thankfully, today there are only a handful of countries where conditions of slavery exist. But enslavement continues. To alcohol, to drugs, to power, to sex, to food. Humans keep discovering new ways to enslave themselves.

In this text the focus is on money. No one can be committed to the accumulation of wealth and to God. In those places where choices have to be made, actual loyalties will emerge.

Beginning in verse 25 through verse 34 is a section that reveals Jesus' own attitude about the extent to which people may put their trust in God. The section aroused great anger among pagans. It was also an object of ridicule. Pagans could not believe that God has such concern for every individual life. Many modern secularists and Christians alike find this passage naive. Nevertheless, this is at the core of Jesus' attitude toward God and toward life.

First, don't be troubled about food and clothing. To be so concerned is typical of people who do not believe there is more to life than the physical. The model for people of faith should be the life of birds. They do not plant or harvest. But God takes care of them. And in the scale of God's values, people are worth more than birds.

Verse 27 is an appeal to people to recognize the limits of their power. Not only can people not add to their lives by worrying, they can cut their lives short and reduce the enjoyment of life itself.

6:28-34

[28] *"And why worry about clothes? Look how the wild flowers grow: they do not work or make clothes for themselves. [29] But I tell you that not even Solomon, as rich as he was, had clothes as beautiful as one of these flowers. [30] It is God who clothes the wild grass — grass that is here today, gone tomorrow, burned up in the oven. Will he not be all the more sure to clothe you? How little is your faith! [31] So do not start worrying: 'Where will my food come from? or my drink? or my clothes?'*

[*32*] [*These are the things the heathen are always after.*] *Your Father in heaven knows that you need all these things.* [*33*] *Instead, give first place to his Kingdom and to what he requires, and he will provide you with all these other things.* [*34*] *So do not worry about tomorrow; it will have enough worries of its own. There is no need to add to the troubles each day brings.*"

The second comparison is to flowers. Lovelier than all of God's creations, grander even than King Solomon dressed for a state occasion, they also flourish for only a very short time. If God lavishes this beauty on objects here for such a short time, surely he will provide clothing for his children.

It is heathen (people who know no loving heavenly father to trust) who worry about such things. But for people of faith such worry is a waste of time and an inversion of values.

For followers of Jesus, concern is to be directed toward God's kingdom and his righteousness, and God will take care of the other things.

All of this advice is not naive, as verse 34 shows. Jesus knows there will be trouble a-plenty. Each new day will have new worries. But the person oriented toward God's kingdom will find that the other things fall into place as well.

Two additional notes ought to be added to this section. First, Jesus directs people's attention to flowers and birds, creatures that contribute primarily to the beauty of the earth but do not work for their keep, except incidentally. Second, this passage is not a guarantee that everything will go well with people in physical terms. But it does say that God will supply our physical needs as long as we have physical life.

Matthew 7

Matthew 7:1-6

[1] *"Do not judge others, so that God will not judge you — [2] because God will judge you in the same way you judge others, and he will apply to you the same rules you apply to others. [3] Why, then, do you look at the speck in your brother's eye, and pay no attention to the log in your own eye? [4] How dare you say to your brother, 'Please, let me take that speck out of your eye,' when you have a log in your own eye? [5] You impostor! Take the log out of your own eye first, and then you will be able to see and take the speck out of your brother's eye.*

[6] "Do not give what is holy to dogs — they will only turn and attack you; do not throw your pearls in front of pigs — they will only trample them underfoot."

The life urged on a Christian is one of non-judgment. Judgment comes easily to people, because one feels let down when someone else fails him. But studies reveal that people are much more ready to forgive themselves than others. Jesus says, by the standard you apply to others, by that standard will you be judged.

Yet people persist in condemning others. Another motive for this self-righteous conduct is that each one seeks to justify himself before God. If he looks better than most of his neighbors, then perhaps God will find him acceptable.

Jesus says rather look to your own weakness. Remove that first and then you will be in a position to help others.

The saying about dogs sounds strange to western ears. In this time dogs are pets. But then they were considered unclean animals. They often traveled in packs, and would be dangerous. Pigs and pearls sound as improbable today as then. Most pigs would give pearls a sniff to see if they might be edible. If not, they would become casualties to the good.

The two sayings do not relate to the material that went before. Rather they are a part of a strong theme that runs in Jesus' preaching. Do not waste important material on an audience that has no respect or concern for it.

7:7-12

[7] *"Ask, and you will receive; seek, and you will find; knock, and the door will be opened to you.* [8] *For everyone who asks will receive, and he who seeks will find, and the door will be opened to him who knocks.* [9] *Would any one of you fathers give his son a stone, when he asks you for bread?* [10] *Or would you give him a snake, when he asks you for fish?* [11] *As bad as you are, you know how to give good things to your children. How much more, then, your Father in heaven will give good things to those who ask him!*

[12] *"Do for others what you want them to do for you: this is the meaning of the Law of Moses and the teaching of the prophets."*

The virtue of persistence is praised in this section. The seeking one will find. The knocking one will be received. The one who asks will receive. Jesus argues from the kindness of parents toward their children to God's own readiness to hear the requests of people, the children of God. He does not have illusions about people. For he says, "if you, bad as you are, know how to give good things to your children."

Verse 12 is the so-called golden rule. Matthew does not present the teaching of Jesus as anything mysterious. The whole Bible, Jesus says, is summed up in this: "do unto others as you wish them to do to you." The context of that saying does not require more than a 50 I.Q. to understand. But it is a challenge to each person to live.

7:13, 14

[13] *"Go in through the narrow gate, for wide and easy is the road that leads to hell, and there are many who travel it.* [14] *The gate is narrow and the way is hard that leads to life, and few people find it."*

Life in this world determines people's fate in the next. The allurements of this world are many: power, money, prestige, admiration, sex. Any of these pursuits — or any number of them — beckon people down the path that leads to destruction. These are lives which are lived for the person, rather than to the glory of God and for others. That road is well traveled, and there one will never lack for companionship.

The road to life is hard and the gate is narrow. The double image, first the entrance to the road and then the road, suggests that there are plenty of ways to slip up even once one is on the road. Certain Christian groups give people the impression that once one is "saved," he no longer needs worry about the state of his soul. But in this saying there is a recognition that people already through the gate will find many things hard on the road. And they may indeed abandon it because of its difficulty.

What then of an easy Christianity? Just pay your church dues and relax. Jesus knows nothing of any such religion.

7:15-20

[15] *"Watch out for false prophets; they come to you looking like sheep on the outside, but they are really like wild wolves on the inside. [16] You will know them by the way they act. Thorn bushes do not bear grapes, and briars do not bear figs. [17] A healthy tree bears good fruit, while a poor tree bears bad fruit. [18] A healthy tree cannot bear bad fruit, and a poor tree cannot bear good fruit. [19] The tree that does not bear good fruit is cut down and thrown in the fire. [20] So, then, you will know the false prophets by the way they act."*

Here Jesus returns to the theme of religious leadership. Every age has had its quota of scalawags, and the last part of the 20th century is no exception. People who speak with authority or with charm can always attract a large following. Ministers, whether on the radio or in the congregation, are sometimes in the business of selling confidence. A question occasionally emerges as to who is the object of that confidence.

Jesus here advises against judgment by appearances. Wait until the person has been around long enough that you can judge his or her works.

The early church eventually had to develop some regulations about traveling prophets, such as "If a person stays for more than three days, he is not a prophet (but a free loader)." "If a person asks for money, he is not a prophet."

Or put another way, "Just because a person is religious doesn't mean he has to be stupid."

7:21-23

[21] "Not every person who calls me 'Lord, Lord,' will enter into the Kingdom of heaven, but only those who do what my Father in heaven wants them to do. [22] When that Day comes, many will say to me, 'Lord, Lord! In your name we told God's message, by your name we drove out many demons and performed many miracles!' [23] Then I will say to them, 'I never knew you. Away from me, you evildoers!' "

Again Jesus emphasizes that lip service alone will not bring membership in the Kingdom of Heaven. The crucial issue is the doing of the will of God.

Jesus also recognizes that preachers, healers, and miracle workers believe themselves to have an inside track. But the answer they receive is without equivocation: "Get out! You were never mine. You are the ones who did works of lawlessness."

7:24-27

[24] "So then, everyone who hears these words of mine and obeys them will be like a wise man who built his house on the rock. [25] The rain poured down, the rivers flooded over, and the winds blew hard against that house. But it did not fall, because it had been built on the rock. [26] Everyone who hears these words of mine and does not obey them will be like a foolish man who built his house on the sand. [27] The rain poured down, the rivers flooded over, the winds blew hard against that house, and it fell. What a terrible fall that was!"

Jesus recognizes two responses to his preaching: the one a response that takes his words to heart and builds upon them; and the other a disregard for what he teaches.

At first there is not a basis for telling the difference between the two, no more difference than if one were to go into a group and attempt to tell the people of faith from those without faith by a casual observation. But when times of testing come, it is then that faith in the God who was before time and who will survive time makes a crucial difference. It is often the difference between a life that falls apart and one that grows through adversity.

The stakes are serious.

7:28-29

[28] Jesus finished saying these things, and the crowds were amazed at the way he taught. [29] He wasn't like their teachers of the Law; instead, he taught with authority.

So ends the Sermon on the Mount. While Luke places the material differently in his Gospel, much of it is shared by Luke. Because Matthew has organized it in such a fashion, it makes Jesus appear as more of a teacher in this Gospel than in the others.

The content impressed the crowds because Jesus represented a new style of teacher. He did not present himself as one whose only role was to interpret the law which God had revealed long ago to Moses. Jesus spoke for God. A characteristic expression he used was, "You have heard that it was said to those of old, but I say unto you." With this phrase he revealed his belief that he could reveal God's law for his kingdom more clearly than it had been revealed in the days of Moses. In his claim to authority, two things must be said.

First, he did not see himself as overthrowing God's law. Matthew includes a quotation in which Jesus affirms it more strongly than in any other biblical book. Jesus did not understand himself as presenting something new, but as something which antedated Moses.

Second, for a person to speak with such authority, he must have understood himself as God's spokesperson. In this way he was both like and different from a prophet. Prophets spoke the word of the Lord. They were mouthpieces. When God gave them nothing to say, they said nothing. Jesus spoke his own words. But he spoke for God. On only one subject did he express reserve, and that was on the timing of the full coming of the kingdom. Otherwise he acted in the now with God's authority.

Finally, what does one make of this sermon? It contains many hard sayings impossible of fulfillment. It is tempting to seek to escape this stern Jesus for the gentler Jesus of picture and song. Yet the words ring with authenticity. They will not disappear. They cannot be institutionalized. Those who have tried to build a society around this law have created cruel parodies of the Kingdom of God. But the challenge of Jesus, this new law, shines like a beacon in the early part of the Gospel. It will not go away. It will not be blotted out. Through it Jesus is continually among us. Larger than church, larger than religion, larger than the easy solutions of theology and ethics. He speaks for God!

Matthew 8

Matthew 8:1-4

[1] Jesus came down from the hill, and large crowds followed him. [2] Then a leper came to him, knelt down before him, and said, "Sir, if you want to, you can make me clean." [3] Jesus reached out and touched him. "I do want to," he answered. "Be clean!" At once he was clean from his leprosy. [4] Then Jesus said to him: "Listen! Don't tell anyone, but go straight to the priest and let him examine you, and then offer the sacrifice that Moses ordered, to prove to everyone that you are now clean."

Jesus was a spectacular healer. If Oral Roberts had had the healing powers of Jesus Christ, he probably would not have gotten into basketball. On this occasion Jesus is to approach a leper. The disease is one of the skin which can be effectively treated today through modern medicine, although it cannot be cured. In the ancient world it was much feared and lepers were forced to live in isolation.

Jesus responded to the leper's faith by agreeing to heal him. He then instructed the leper to prove his health to the priest and to offer a sacrifice of thanksgiving according to the Law of Moses. The odd note is his instruction not to tell anyone about the healing. It seems that he did not want to make a reputation as a healer.

8:5-13

[5] When Jesus entered Capernaum, a Roman officer met him and begged for help: [6] "Sir, my servant is home sick in bed, unable to move, and suffering terribly." [7] "I will go and make him well," Jesus said. [8] "Oh no, sir," answered the officer. "I do not deserve to have you come into my house. Just give the order and my servant will get well. [9] I, too, am a man with superior officers over me, and I have soldiers under me; so I order this one, 'Go!' and he goes; and I order that one, 'Come!' and he comes; and I order my slave, 'Do this!' and he does it." [10] Jesus was surprised when he heard this, and said to the people who were following him: "I tell you, I have never seen such faith as this in anyone in Israel. [11] Remember this! Many will come from the east and the west and sit down at the table in the Kingdom of heaven with Abraham, Isaac, and Jacob. [12 But those who should be in the Kingdom will be thrown out into the darkness outside, where they will cry and gnash their teeth." [13] And Jesus said to the officer, "Go home, and what you believe will be done for you." And the officer's servant was healed that very hour.

57

Jesus apparently had taken residence in Capernaum. The presence of a Roman officer there points to the presence of a Roman garrison. The man may have already known of the special qualities of Jesus when he came asking on behalf of his servant (or son; the word **pais** can mean either). Jesus quickly agreed to his request to heal the servant, and said that he would come.

But the officer, conscious of Jesus' holiness, declined to have him come to his house. He instead urged Jesus to simply give the word, and the healing would be accomplished.

Jesus was surprised to discover such faith from a Gentile. It led to his exclamation that when the roll is called up yonder, there will be people from the entire world and not simply Jews sitting with Abraham, Isaac, and Jacob. And on the other side, many who expect to be there will be left outside. The same idea, of course, applies to Christians who imagine themselves to have an automatic pass to the messianic banquet because they know the name of Jesus Christ.

The request for a healing was honored. Jesus assured the officer that his servant would be healed. And it was accomplished. This is one of the few New Testament healings at a distance.

8:14-17

[14] *Jesus went to Peter's home, and there he saw Peter's mother-in-law sick in bed with a fever. [15] He touched her hand; the fever left her, and she got up and began to wait on him.*

[16] *When evening came, people brought to Jesus many who had demons in them. Jesus drove out the evil spirits with a word and healed all who were sick. [17] He did this to make come true what the prophet Isaiah had said, "He himself took our illnesses and carried away our diseases."*

Another spectacular healing is worked, this time on Peter's mother-in-law. (This is how it is known that Jesus' chief apostle was married.) Not only was she healed but she felt so much better she was able to entertain guests.

Verse 16 casually introduces the fact that Jesus did

exorcisms as well as healings. Exorcisms will be discussed later as individual ones are reported. Here they are reported as a portion of Jesus' ministry to alleviate human suffering. Matthew understands Jesus' healing as a fulfillment of Isaiah 53:4.

8:18-22

[18] Jesus noticed the crowd around him and gave orders to go to the other side of the lake. [19] A teacher of the Law came to him. "Teacher," he said, "I am ready to go with you wherever you go." [20] Jesus answered him, "Foxes have holes, and birds have nests, but the Son of Man has no place to lie down and rest." [21] Another man, who was a disciple, said, "Sir, first let me go and bury my father." [22] "Follow me," Jesus answered, "and let the dead bury their own dead."

Jesus shrank from those who were interested in him for what he could accomplish for human betterment. Since he acted to heal people, he certainly did not oppose it. What he seemed to oppose was an understanding that saw it as the basic meaning of his vocation.

Conditions of discipleship were stringent. The rabbi who wished to follow him was warned that Jesus had no regular accommodations. A man who wished time off to bury his father was rebuked.

Jesus apparently had more disciples than the twelve, and the number may have been greater and lesser at various times.

8:23-27

[23] Jesus got into the boat, and his disciples went with him. [24] Suddenly a fierce storm hit the lake, so that the waves covered the boat. But Jesus was asleep. [25] The disciples went to him and woke him up. "Save us, Lord!" they said. "We are about to die!" [26] "Why are you so frightened?" Jesus answered. "How little faith you have!" Then he got up and gave a command to the winds and to the waves, and there was a great calm. [27] Everyone was amazed. "What kind of man is this?" they said. "Even the winds and the waves obey him!"

Jesus was at home on the Sea of Galilee. He must have regarded it as a friendly lake (although fierce storms could blow up quickly) to have been able to sleep when waves were dashing upon the boat.

It is hard to imagine anyone not being frightened

under such circumstances. The Sea of Galilee is a big lake. And in rough seas a swimmer would not last long. They feared for their lives, a healthy human fear with which most can identify.

But Jesus was as surprised by their lack of faith as he had been impressed by the faith of the Roman officer. He stirred himself awake, and commanded the wind and the waves to be still. A command to the wind would probably have been sufficient. The waves could not have kept up long without wind.

When this happened the disciples knew they were up against someone really special. It was one thing to be able to heal. But to have command of the elements as well was another.

8:28-34

[28] *Jesus came to the territory of the Gadarenes, on the other side of the lake, and was met by two men who came out of the burial caves. These men had demons in them and were very fierce, so dangerous that no one dared travel on that road. [29] At once they screamed, "What do you want with us, Son of God? Have you come to punish us before the right time?" [30] Not far away a large herd of pigs was feeding. [31] The demons begged Jesus, "If you are going to drive us out, send us into that herd of pigs." [32] "Go," Jesus told them; so they left and went off into the pigs. The whole herd rushed down the side of the cliff into the lake and were drowned.*

[33] *The men who had been taking care of the pigs ran away and went to the town, where they told the whole story, and what had happened to the men with the demons. [34] So everybody from that town went out to meet Jesus; and when they saw him they begged him to leave their territory.*

The trip on the boat brought Jesus into non-Jewish territory, whether by force of wind or design is not told. Clearly it is Gentile territory, since Jews would not be raising pigs.

What he encountered there were men (a man, according to Mark) possessed by demons. They apparently would attack people who passed that way.

A question raised by this story must be dealt with immediately. The point of view represented here is that demons (bodiless spirits) can take control of people and bring them to act in all kinds of irrational ways. This is strange to many modern people who have been led to believe that the only realities in the world are physical realities. But such a point of view is unnecessarily narrow. The universe is occupied by a variety of spiritual beings as well. Among these spiritual beings are demons, good-for-nothings that enjoy making life miserable. Given half a chance they will control a person.

When the men saw Jesus, the demons in them cried out. They cried out because they recognized Jesus as a mortal enemy. Their question ("Have you come here to trouble us before the appropriate time?") reveals their recognition of Jesus as Son of God and their belief that the Kingdom of Heaven would not enter the world until the end of time.

Jesus turned out not only to be tough on demons, but tough on business. His leniency in allowing the demons to enter the pigs set in motion a series of events that led the pig farmers to urge Jesus to leave their territory. Two men restored to wholeness did not count much when compared with lost revenue on drowned pigs. The world has not changed much.

Matthew 9

Matthew 9:1-8

*[1] Jesus got into the boat, went back across the lake, and came to his
own town. [2] Some people brought him a paralyzed man, lying on a bed.
Jesus saw how much faith they had, and said to the paralyzed man,
"Courage, my son! Your sins are forgiven." [3] Then some teachers of the
Law said to themselves, "This man is talking against God!" [4] Jesus
knew what they were thinking and said: "Why are you thinking such evil
things? [5] Is it easier to say, 'Your sins are forgiven,' or to say, 'Get up
and walk'? [6] I will prove to you, then, that the Son of Man has authority
on earth to forgive sins." So he said to the paralyzed man, "Get up, pick
up your bed, and go home!" [7] The man got up and went home. [8] When
the people saw it, they were afraid, and praised God for giving such
authority as this to men.*

Jesus could take a hint. He left and went back to
Capernaum. On this occasion he is attacked by leaders
because he healed the man by pronouncing his forgiveness. They accuse him of blasphemy. Blasphemy in this
case would be that of a man presuming to speak for God
by forgiving sins.

The answer of Jesus to the charge is twofold. First,
he insisted that there is a kind of identity between
healing and forgiving. This insistence that there is an
inevitable connection between things physical and things
spiritual offends many. People of all stripes wish to
clearly separate between things of religion and matters
of national well being.

The second part of Jesus' answer reveals that he
understood himself in terms of one of the most exalted
figures in the Old Testament, the Son of man. This
figure, foreseen in Daniel as a figure at the end time, is
magnificent, a cloud rider. In John 1:51 he is so big that
angels can go up into heaven and down from heaven upon
him.

Jesus claimed identity with the Son of man. The Son
of man had been expected at the end of time. Judgment
— condemnation and forgiveness — was expected at the
end of time. Jesus in this passage claims authority as Son
of man to forgive in the present. This evidence links up
with Jesus' preaching that the Kingdom of God is near.

And it led many to believe the nearness of the end of the
world.

The man was healed. The crowd was awed. They
knew something new was afoot in the world when a man
among them commanded so much authority.

9:9-13

[9] *Jesus left that place, and as he walked along he saw a tax
collector, named Matthew, sitting in his office. He said to him, "Follow
me." And Matthew got up and followed him.*

[10] *While Jesus was having dinner at his house, many tax collectors
and outcasts came and joined him and his disciples at the table.* [11]
*Some Pharisees saw this and said to his disciples, "Why does your
teacher eat with tax collectors and outcasts?"* [12] *Jesus heard them and
answered: "People who are well do not need a doctor, but only those who
are sick.* [13] *Go and find out what this scripture means, 'I do not want
animal sacrifices, but kindness.' For I have not come to call the
respectable people, but the outcasts."*

This story is a particularly meaningful one for this
Gospel, for it is the account of the call of the man for
whom the Gospel is named. (In the parallel accounts in
Mark and Luke the disciple is called Levi.)

In the incident itself, however the name of the man is
not so important as his occupation. Judaism considered
certain vocations unclean, and the people who occupied
them unfit for association with righteous people. If the
righteous did associate with them they were themselves
polluted by the proximity. The same matter of table
fellowship (this time between Jews and Gentiles) comes
up in Galatians.

Tax collectors were a special case because they were
representing a foreign power of occupation.

Some Pharisees questioned Jesus' association with
tax collectors and sinners. The challenge provided Jesus
an opportunity to interpret his own mission. He did not
come to help those who need no help, but to minister to
the sick. The involvement with the outcasts was not
incidental, but central to his work. Hosea 6:6 is quoted to
indicate that in focusing on ministry rather than purity
Jesus is consistent with the Scriptures.

9:14-17

[14] Then the followers of John the Baptist came to Jesus, asking, "Why is it that we and the Pharisees fast often, but your disciples don't fast at all?" [15] Jesus answered: "Do you expect the guests at a wedding party to be sad as long as the bridegroom is withthem? Of course not! But the time will come when the bridegroom will be taken away from them, and then they will go without food.

[16] "No one patches up an old coat with a piece of new cloth; for such a patch tears off from the coat, making an even bigger hole. [17] Nor does anyone pour new wine into used wineskins. If he does, the skins will burst, and then the wine pours out and the skins will be ruined. Instead, new wine is poured into fresh wineskins, and both will keep in good condition."

The question of fasting re-emerges, this time as a contrast between the disciples of John the Baptizer and the Pharisees on the one side and the disciples of Jesus on the other. The grouping itself is interesting in that it shows that in this period there were no clean breaks between the various groups, but a variety of ways of attempting to be faithful to the God of Israel.

The question, if one judged by present Protestant practice, might have been expected to be answered in some way that rejected fasting. But Jesus answered in a way that seems to say that during his ministry his disciples would not fast, but when he was taken away, they would fast. It is not clear whether this meant just for the three days of his death or if it applied to the period after his earthly ministry.

The passage beginning with verse 16 may testify to the state of things in the era before "pre-shrunk." A new patch on an old garment may shrink at washing while the old garment has no more elasticity. Result: a new tear. The reference to wineskins is similar. New wine will carbonate and expand. Old wineskins will have already expanded to their capacity. If one places new in old, both will be lost.

As with all of Jesus' parables, it is left to the hearer to determine what his comment applies to. Perhaps it means that the implications of Jesus' ministry are so great that it will not simply mean modern adjustments for the Judaism of that time.

64

9:18-22

[18] *While Jesus was saying this to them, a Jewish official came to him, knelt down before him, and said, "My daughter has just died; but come and place your hand on her and she will live."*

[19] *So Jesus got up and followed him, and his disciples went with him.*

[20] *A certain woman, who had had severe bleeding for twelve years, came up behind Jesus and touched the edge of his cloak. [21] She said to herself, "If only I touch his cloak I will get well."*

[22] *Jesus turned around and saw her, and said, "Courage, my daughter! Your faith has made you well." At that very moment the woman became well.*

This is a case of a healing within another miracle story. While on his way to raise the daughter of an official from the dead, a woman had such confidence in his power that she touched his garment to gain healing. Stories of healing through contact with a garment or image of a holy person are common enough. Such was done with handkerchiefs and aprons used by Paul as reported in Acts 19:12. North America's most recently proclaimed saint is credited with healings which resulted from contact with his pictures.

In Mark's version of this story the woman is healed before Jesus knew what happened, indicating the kind of combination set up by his power and her desire. For whatever reason, Matthew did not tell the same version of the story, but has the woman's healing await Jesus' acknowledgment of her presence.

9:23-26

[23] *So Jesus went into the official's house. When he saw the musicians for the funeral, and the people all stirred up, [24] he said, "Get out, everybody! The little girl is not dead — she is only sleeping!"*

They all started making fun of him. [25] As soon as the people had been put out, Jesus went into the girl's room and took hold of her hand, and she got up. [26] The news about this spread all over that part of the country.

The second miracle is one of the more spectacular of Jesus' healings, the raising of a person already dead. The scene is quite vivid. The funeral, a same day affair without embalming, was already in process at Jesus' arrival. His insistence that she was only sleeping makes him an object of ridicule to the people present — perhaps it was a nervous laughter initially, but it turned into ridicule.

One of the unusual features of this story is the fact that Jesus is seen as an object of laughter. The same occurs when he is on the cross. A great deal has been made of Jesus recently as a person with a sense of humor. No doubt he had, in that some of his stories have a humorous side. But there is no mention in the New Testament of his laughing, only being laughed at. He knew ridicule, but he did not ridicule others.

And it was worth it in that the girl was returned to her father.

9:27-31

[27] *Jesus left that place, and as he walked along two blind men started following him. "Have mercy on us, Son of David!" they shouted.*

[28] *When Jesus had gone indoors, the two blind men came to him and he asked them, "Do you believe that I can do this?"*

"Yes, sir!" they answered.

[29] *Then Jesus touched their eyes and said, "May it happen, then, just as you believe!" —* [30] *and their sight was restored. Jesus spoke harshly to them, "Don't tell this to anyone!"*

[31] *But they left and spread the news about Jesus all over that part of the country.*

In this story the point is again made of the requirement of faith for the consummation of the miracle. The faith need be in more than a belief that the miracle can happen. Of course a belief that good can come in the world is a sign of belief in the direction of the world.

Again those healed are warned not to tell anyone of the healing. And again Jesus' command was not observed. The men spread the news of what had happened to them.

Why Jesus did not wish his cures to be known is not told. Perhaps he did not wish to make a reputation as a healer, in that to understand him simply as a healer would be to misunderstand him.

66

9:32-34

[32] *As the men were leaving, some people brought to Jesus a man who could not talk because he had a demon. [33] As soon as the demon was driven out, the man started talking. Everyone was amazed. "We never saw the like in Israel!" they exclaimed.*

[34] *But the Pharisees said, "It is the chief of the demons who gives him the power to drive them out."*

Jews recognized illnesses that were physical and those that were spiritual. Some spiritual illnesses had physical manifestations. One of the latter was the mute who was brought to Jesus. Demon-possessed people who had some physical manifestation are often diagnosed today as having hysteric or psychosomatic conditions. The ancient world understood this to be linked to a soul disturbance (**psyche**) or imbalance (**hysteria**). The modern age, having lost contact with soul language, has had success dealing with the condition through drugs, shock treatment, and therapy.

Jesus' power over demons was suspect in his time. Exorcism has always aroused certain uneasiness, because it involves communication with evil spirits. Some Pharisees claimed that Jesus did not do this through God's power, but through the chief of the demons. This issue arises again later in the ministry of Jesus.

9:35-38

[35] *So Jesus went around visiting all the towns and villages. He taught in their synagogues, preached the Good News of the Kingdom, and healed people from every kind of disease and sickness. [36] As he saw the crowds, his heart was filled with pity for them, because they were worried and helpless, like sheep without a shepherd. [37] So he said to his disciples, "There is a large harvest, but few workers to gather it in. [38] Pray to the owner of the harvest that he will send out workers to gather in his harvest."*

Jesus did not limit his ministry to a particular place, but visited all the towns and villages around. He came into the synagogues, preaching his message of the Kingdom of God. He also continued his ministry of healing.

Verse 36 reveals the orientation of his healing ministry. He had such compassion for the people that he reached out to them. Yet his direction was to bring people to the point where they could help themselves.

His comment to the disciples that there is a great harvest but few workers is still true of the world. Simply one could say that there are three groups in the world: the takers, the helpers, and the victims. The smallest group is the helpers. There is plenty of work to do, both in evangelism and in the alleviation of physical needs. But there are not enough people to do the work. Jesus urges his followers to ask that the number of workers might be increased.

68

Matthew 10

10:1-4

[1] Jesus called his twelve disciples together and gave them authority to drive out the evil spirits and to heal every disease and every sickness. These are the names of the twelve apostles: first, Simon [called Peter] and hs brother Andrew; James and his brother John, the sons of Zebedee; [3] Philip and Bartholomew; Thomas and Matthew, the tax collector; James, the son of Alphaeus, and Thaddaeus; [4] Simon the Patriot, and Judas Iscariot, who betrayed Jesus.

This is the first list of Jesus' disciples in this Gospel. It is the only Gospel that identifies Matthew as a tax collector. Together with Mark it identifies the tenth disciple as Thaddaeus, while Luke has Judas the son of James.

The disciples are given authority to cast out demons and to heal. They are enabled to do this in Jesus' name.

10:5-15

[5] Jesus sent these twelve men out with the following instructions: "Do not go to any Gentile territory or any Samaritan towns. [6] Go, instead, to the lost sheep of the people of Israel. [7] Go and preach, 'The Kingdom of heaven is near!' [8] Heal the sick, raise the dead, make the lepers clean, drive out demons. You have received without paying, so give without being paid. [9] Do not carry any gold, silver, or copper money in your pockets; [10] do not carry a beggar's bag for the trip, or an extra shirt, or shoes, or a walking stick. A worker should be given what he needs.

[11] "When you come to a town or village, go in and look for someone who is willing to welcome you, and stay with him until you leave that place. [12] When you go into a house say, 'Pleace be with you.' [13] If the people in that house welcome you, let your greeting of peace remain; but if they do not welcome you, then take back your greeting. [14] And if some home or town will not welcome you or listen to you, then leave that place and shake the dust off your feet. [15] Remember this! On the Judgment Day God will show more mercy to the people of Sodom and Gomorrah than to the people of that town!"

The sending out of the Twelve on a mission during Jesus' own ministry gave them an opportunity to practice while they were still in study with him. That the circumstances are different from those in the later church is indicated by the restriction to a Jewish audience. Both Gentiles, who are later included in the

Christian mission, and Samaritans are excluded. Samaritans were suspect because they had not shared in the Babylonian exile and because they continued to worship at traditional holy places and had not agreed to the centralization of worship in Jerusalem.

The acts of healing, raising the dead, leper cleansing, and demon exorcism seem to be the carrying out of the proclamation of the Kingdom of God.

Jesus shows special concern for the physical and financial arrangements of their mission. They are not to personally profit from their work. But they are also not to become beggars. The place they go ought to provide their support.

The imperial nature of their mission is indicated by the way the response of the visited towns is described. The disciples may bless if they are given a favorable reception, or curse, if they are not. The time is decisive. And the place that rejects has chosen a place on judgment day worse than the sin cities of Sodom and Gomorrah.

10:16-25

[16] "Listen! I am sending you just like sheep to a pack of wolves. You must be as cautious as snakes and as gentle as doves. [17] Watch out, for there will be men who will arrest you and take you to court, and they will whip you in their synagogues. [18] You will be brought to trial before rulers and kings for my sake, to tell the Good News to them and to the Gentiles. [19] When they bring you to trial, do not worry about what you are going to say or how you will say it; when the time comes, you will be given what you will say. [20] For the words you speak will not be yours; they will come from the Spirit of your Father speaking in you.

[21] "Men will hand over their own brothers to be put to death, and fathers will do the same to their children; children will turn against their parents and have them put to death. [22] Everyone will hate you, because of me. But whoever holds out to the end will be saved. [23] And when they persecute you in one town, run away to another one. I tell you, you will not finish your work in all the towns of Israel before the Son of Man comes.

[24] "No pupil is greater than his teacher; no slave is greater than his master. If the head of the family is called Beelzebul, the members of the family will be called by even worse names!"

Jesus knew that he was sending his disciples on a

suicide mission, "sheep among wolves," he says. They are to be wise as serpents and gentle as doves. This double advice indicates that followers need not be stupid, only that they are not to use violence in the attainment of their purposes.

The proclamation will bring arrest. And arrest will bring opportunity to testify before rulers. At such a point the Holy Spirit provides appropriate language. It seems as if the courts of princes and kings is an appropriate place for the gospel to be challenged.

Verse 21 accurately predicts what would become the situation in Judaism, and what would be repeated in later Christianity any number of times. At this point, however, the focus is entirely on a near expectation of the end of time. In retrospect it is known that the full coming did not happen. The Son of Man is still to come in glory.

Verse 24 is a reminder that Christians are not asked to do any more, or less, than Jesus. Christians are students of Jesus, slaves to Jesus. If even he was ridiculed and called the devil, what then can the followers expect?

10:26-31

[26] *"Do not be afraid of men, then. Whatever is covered up will be uncovered, and every secret will be made known. [27] What I am telling you in the dark you must repeat in broad daylight, and what you have heard in private you must tell from the housetops. [28] Do not be afraid of those who kill the body but cannot kill the soul; rather be afraid of God, who can destroy both body and soul in hell. [29] You can buy two sparrows for a penny; yet not a single one of them falls to the ground without your Father's consent. [30] As for you, even the hairs of your head have been counted. [31] So do not be afraid; you are worth much more than many sparrows!"*

The proper object of fear is not people. It is easy enough to live life intimidated by the people around one: bosses, parents, teachers. The person to fear is Satan. He is the one who has the power to cast the soul into Hades.

The focus so clearly delineated here in verse 28 is

often forgotten in the modern world. The thing of ultimate worth and ultimate responsibility that each person has is his or her own soul. Men or machines may destroy the body. Many a tragic accident has cut off a life long before the lapse of the normal threescore and ten. Such deaths are truly tragic. Almost inconsolable for those who are left behind.

But it is the soul that must be guarded. It cannot be harmed by physical attack. But it is vulnerable to drugs, alcohol, sexism, Satanism, materialism.

The good news is that God is the ultimate power. And he is so wrapped up with life that not even a bird falls unknown to him. Christian courage grows out of an awareness that the physical world is not all that there is and a confidence in the love and providence of God.

10:32-33

[32] *"Whoever declares publicly that he belongs to me, I will do the same for him before my Father in heaven. [33] But whoever denies publicly that he belongs to me, then I will deny him before my Father in heaven."*

The linkage of earthly to heavenly fate is again reasserted. Public affirmation of Jesus on earth results in heavenly affirmation of the person before the Father. Public denial of Jesus on earth results in heavenly denial of the person before God.

This saying in particular underlines the ultimate significance of earthly life.

10:34-39

[34] *"Do not think that I have come to bring peace to the world; no, I did not come to bring peace, but a sword. [35] I came to set sons against their fathers, daughters against their mothers, daughters-in law against their mothers-in-law; [36] a man's worst enemies will be the members of his own family.*

[37] *"Whoever loves his father or mother more than me is not worthy of me; whoever loves his son or daughter more than me is not worthy of me. [38] Whoever does not take up his cross and follow in my steps is not worthy of me. [39] Whoever tries to gain his own life will lose it; whoever loses his life for my sake will gain it."*

Jesus was by and large a peaceful person while on

earth. But his message did not make for peace and it does not make for peace. It involves the individual or community caught up in it in God's struggle for righteousness.

Immediately a commitment to such a struggle puts one in tension with those people who only wish to "eat, drink, and make merry for tomorrow we die." And some of those so committed will be members of one's own family. Their given song or normality will be a negative influence for the follower of Jesus.

Jesus, as verse 37 indicates, demands first place. Parents and children cannot take his place. Nor can the Christian shrink from meeting his/her own responsibilities in the world. Jesus had his cross. Each of his followers will have one of his/her own.

Verse 39 points to a profound mystery of life, revealed in Jesus Christ. It is only when one lets go that he/she discovers life. When one tries to clutch it in the first place, it is lost.

10:40-42

[40] *"Whoever welcomes you, welcomes me; and whoever welcomes me, welcomes the one who sent me. [41] Whoever welcomes God's messenger because he is God's messenger will share in his reward; and whoever welcomes a truly good man, because he is that, will share in his reward. [42] And remember this! Whoever gives even a drink of cold water to one of the least of these my followers, because he is my follower, will certainly receive his reward."*

A humbling message is contained in this section. The disciple of Jesus is his emissary. Who receives him, receives Jesus, receives God. This makes for a deep sense of awe in human relationships regardless of which side one is on. Each person should treat every other with the reverence one would show for God.

Further, reward awaits the one who treats Jesus' followers with the dignity due God. This passage is a clue to the kind of dignity people ought to have from God's perspective.

Matthew 11

11:1-6

[1] *When Jesus finished giving these instructions to his twelve disciples, he left that place and went on to teach and preach in the towns near there.*

[2] *When John the Baptist heard in prison about Christ's works, he sent some of his disciples to him.* [3] *"Tell us," they asked Jesus, "are you the one John said was going to come, or should we expect someone else?"*

[4] *Jesus answered, "Go back and tell John what you are hearing and seeing:* [5] *the blind can see, the lame can walk, the lepers are made clean, the deaf hear, the dead are raised to life, and the Good News is preached to the poor.* [6] *How happy is he who has no doubts about me!"*

The brief mention of Jesus' preaching and teaching in surrounding towns is a reminder of the great amount of teaching which is not recorded in the New Testament.

The question of John's disciples — which John must surely have suggested that they ask — is an illustration of the reliability of the Bible. Here is the forerunner of the Messiah, whose very purpose had been to prepare his way, indicating that his time in prison (and perhaps reports about Jesus) had given him reason to inquire whether Jesus is in fact the Christ. Nothing could be more natural, given the difference in approach and personality, between the two. Yet precious little in modern religion approaches the simple humanity of John's doubts on this occasion, conveyed through his disciples.

Jesus did not seem offended by the question. He pointed to his actions, which coincide to the promise of deliverance in Isaiah 61. He was wise enough to know that if one is doubted it does no good to ask for trust, but it does make sense to point to the record.

What Jesus pointed to to confirm his Messiahship are acts that every decent human being would applaud. The first four acts are today most frequently accomplished through the agency of physicians, whose work is universally admired. The raising of the dead — where it can be accomplished — is also admired by all. It is only on the preaching of good news that humanity finds occasion to argue. Yet Jesus saw it as consistent with his healings, and no less important. Note that the poor are the focus of the preaching. Even here Christian proclamation has social implications.

Verse 6 could be better translated, "Blessed is he who is not scandalized by me." Jesus did not wish to call attention to himself, but to his work. And if people could be scandalized by Jesus, how much more by other preachers. It is good advice to all to look at the accomplishments rather than to be put off by the style.

11:7-15

[7] While John's disciples were going back, Jesus spoke about John to the crowds, "When you went out to John in the desert, what did you expect to see? A blade of grass bending in the wind? [8] What did you go out to see? A man dressed up in fancy clothes? People who dress like that live in palaces! [9] Tell me, what did you go out to see? A prophet? Yes, I tell you — you saw much more than a prophet. [10] For John is the one of whom the scripture says: 'Here is my messenger, says God; I will send him ahead of you to open the way for you.' [11] Remember this! John the Baptist is greater than any man who has ever lived. But he who is least in the Kingdom of heaven is greater than he. [12] From the time John preached his message until this very day the Kingdom of heaven has suffered violent attacks, and violent men try to seize it. [13] All the prophets and the Law of Moses, until the time of John, spoke about the Kingdom; [14] and if you are willing to believe their message, John is Elijah, whose coming was predicted. [15] Listen, then, if you have ears!

Jesus' evaluation of John is one of the longest sustained speeches of Jesus in the entire Gospel. It is a response to John's wondering about who Jesus is.

There was a great tide of expectation in the time of Jesus. Here Jesus' own view (as organized by Matthew) is presented.

The aim is the Kingdom of God. The Law of Moses and the Prophets spoke of it. John is greater than either Moses or the prophets. He is a bridge figure to the Kingdom. Thus Jesus can say that he is greater than anyone who had gone before. Yet the least in the Kingdom of heaven is greater.

He also cites Malachi 3:1 in calling John a messenger (10). Further, Jesus calls John Elijah, probably citing Malachi 4:5, where Elijah is predicted as forerunner to the day of the Lord. Some argue that this identification of John with Elijah makes Jesus a believer in reincarnation. It is perhaps more likely that John was a figure like Elijah. Elijah had enough of his own continuing identity to appear with Jesus and Moses in Matthew 17:3.

Throughout this passage Jesus indicates his great admiration for John.

11:16-19

[16] "Now, to what can I compare the people of this day? They are like children sitting in the market place. One group shouts to the other, [17] 'We played wedding music for you, but you would not dance! We sang funeral songs, but you would not cry!' [18] John came, and he fasted and drank no wine, and everyone said, 'He has a demon in him!' [19] The Son of Man came, and he ate and drank, and everyone said, 'Look at this man! He is a glutton and wine-drinker, a friend of tax collectors and outcasts!' God's wisdom, however, is shown to be true by its results."

The subject of John fascinated Jesus, apparently because their difference in styles — and their uniqueness — became an occasion for rejecting the new and therefore their message.

Neither John nor Jesus conformed to societal expectations. John was too religious for the secular and Jesus was too secular for the religious. Jesus, however, urged that they both be judged not on their style (drinking or teetotaling), but on their results!

11:20-24

[20] Then Jesus began to reproach the towns where he had performed most of his miracles, because the people had not turned from their sins. [21] "How terrible it will be for you, Chorazin! How terrible for you too, Bethsaida! If the miracles which were performed in you had been performed in Tyre and Sidon, long ago the people there would have put on sackcloth, and sprinkled ashes on themselves to show they had turned from their sins! [22] Remember, then, that on the Judgment Day God will show more mercy to the people of Tyre and Sidon than to you! [23] And as for you, Capernaum! You wanted to lift yourself up to heaven? You will be thrown down to hell! If the miracles which were performed in you had been performed in Sodom, it would still be in existence today! [24] Remember, then, that on the Judgment Day God will show more mercy to Sodom than to you!"

The weight of responsibility upon those who have heard the gospel is one of the heavier themes of Jesus' preaching. He compared them to three wicked cities, Sodom, which God destroyed because of its aberrant (homosexual) sexual practices, and Tyre and Sidon, cities in Jesus' own time.

The sins of Chorazin and Bethsaida, towns north of the Sea of Galilee, are not mentioned. Capernaum, the city of Jesus' residence, is accused of pride. But in all three cases, the chief sin is lost opportunity. The kind of witness — of word and miracle — should have made for the repentance of those towns. But it did not. It is this single fact that marks them as wicked.

Such a warning continues for each person and community which has known the power of God in the gospel of Jesus Christ.

11:25-27

[25] *At that time Jesus said, "Father, Lord of heaven and earth! I thank you because you have shown to the unlearned what you have hidden from the wise and learned. [26] Yes, Father, this was done by your own choice and pleasure.*

[27] *"My Father has given me all things. No one knows the Son except the Father, and no one knows the Father except the Son, and those to whom the Son wants to reveal him."*

The prayer in verses 25-26 is one of the few prayers of Jesus recorded in the New Testament. While he withdraws for prayer many times, those prayers remain private. This one is private, too; but the reader is allowed to listen in.

The theme is one which is reported often in Christian theology, that of God's revelation to the simple instead of to the learned. Paul loudly criticizes the wisdom of this world; Martin Luther in exasperation referred to reason as a whore.

Jesus may have been referring to himself, in that he did not have much formal education. More likely, however, he was moved by the fact that the simple of his day responded much more favorably to his message.

The hiding from the wise and learned is not explained in the prayer. One may speculate that the learned person's pride in his own solutions to the riddles of the world makes him less open to the movings of God. But the prayer itself only says it was God's good pleasure so to do. A comfort of the prayer is that there is no minimum I.Q. for a relationship to God.

Verse 27 is striking because in it Jesus speaks exactly as he does throughout the Gospel of John of his social relationship to God. Normally in the three synoptic gospels (Matthew, Mark, Luke) Jesus says very little about that dimension.

11:28-30

[28] *"Come to me, all of you who are tired from carrying your heavy loads, and I will give you rest. [29] Take my yoke and put it on you, and learn from me, because I am gentle and humble in spirit; and you will find rest. [30] The yoke I will give you is easy, and the load I will put on you is light."*

This is perhaps the most beautiful statement of Jesus in the gospel. Matthew understands Jesus as the preacher of a new law. But it is not with a spirit of anger or hardness. In contrast to the difficult burdens of life, Jesus' yoke (the wooden frame an ox wears) is easy.

This passage provides a context for understanding other sayings of Jesus. It is certainly true that he has requirements, but they are laid on in a spirit of gentleness and love. And they are a yoke that leads to life.

Matthew 12

12:1-8

[1] Not long afterward Jesus was walking through the wheat fields on a Sabbath day. His disciples were hungry, so they began to pick heads of wheat and eat the grain. [2] When the Pharisees saw this, they said to Jesus, "Look, it is against our Law for your disciples to do this on the Sabbath!"

[3] Jesus answered, "Have you never read what David did that time when he and his men were hungry? [4] He went into the house of God, and he and his men ate the bread offered to God, even though it was against the Law for them to eat that bread — only the priests were allowed to eat it. [5] Or have you not read in the Law of Moses that every Sabbath the priests in the temple actually break the Sabbath law, yet they are not guilty? [6] There is something here, I tell you, greater than the temple. [7] The scripture says, 'I do not want animal sacrifices, but kindness.' If you really knew what this means, you would not condemn people who are not guilty; [8] because the Son of Man is Lord of the Sabbath."

This particular controversy story belongs to a group which indicates that Jesus did not take observance of the Sabbath (Saturday) in the same way the Old Testament and the religious Jews of Jesus' own day did. When his disciples were criticized in this story for harvesting on the Sabbath, he defended them by appeal to the action of David (1 Samuel 21:1-6).

The story reveals one element of Jesus' radical revision of Mosaic Judaism. The Judaism of Jesus' day was organized around a distinctive people, the temple, and the Law. Jesus' casualness about these matters made for an inevitable conflict with the religious authorities of his day.

What he stood for was the priority of human need over religious discipline. That does not mean that he had no concern for discipline, only that to a leadership preoccupied with discipline he emphasized human need.

12:9-14

[9] Jesus left that place and went to one of their synagogues. [10] A man was there who had a crippled hand. There were some men present who wanted to accuse Jesus of wrongdoing; so they asked him, "Is it against our Law to cure on the Sabbath?"

[11] *Jesus answered, "What if one of you has a sheep and it falls into a deep hole on the Sabbath? Will you not take hold of it and lift it out?* [12] *And a man is worth much more than a sheep! So then, our Law does allow us to help someone on the Sabbath."* [13] *Then he said to the man, "Stretch out your hand."*

He stretched it out, and it became well again, just like the other one. [14] *The Pharisees left and made plans against Jesus to kill him.*

For some reason, the "Good News" translators chose to describe the person healed by Jesus as a man with a paralyzed hand. In Greek, the hand is described as withered, dried, atrophied. The original cause may have been paralysis, but the muscles had deteriorated considerably in the meantime.

For the man healed, the cure was obviously the best day of his life. But the story was remembered and retold because of the Sabbath controversy. If it had happened any other day of the week, there would have been no problem. On this day, however, Jews were not to labor. And to heal was to labor.

Jesus put the argument to his opponents by a reference to the tradition that allowed for the saving of animals. Since people are more important than animals, it followed in this thinking that the man should be healed. Had his opponents been given opportunity to answer, they would have said that since the man had survived with that condition for some years, he could easily wait until the next day.

The leadership saw very clearly that there was a fundamental difference in point of view between them and Jesus. And they determined to do away with him.

12:15-21

[15] *When Jesus heard about it, he went away from that place; and many people followed him. He healed all the sick,* [16] *and gave them orders not to tell others about him,* [17] *to make come true what God had said through the prophet Isaiah,*

[18] *"Here is my servant, whom I have chosen,*
    the one I love, with whom I am well pleased.
    I will put my Spirit on him,
    and he will announce my judgment to all peoples.
[19] *But he will not argue or shout,*
    nor make loud speeches in the streets.

[20] *He will not break off a bent reed,*
    nor put out a flickering lamp.
    He will persist until he causes justice to triumph;
[21] *and all people will put their hope in him."*

In this case it is Matthew the evangelist who provides the interpretation of Jesus through the prophecy of Isaiah. It is not at all surprising that early theologians saw Jesus in the servant passages of Isaiah, because the parallels are striking.

In the passage, the servant is characterized as having a quiet strength. He was not loud but his quietness should not be mistaken for cowardice. When confronted he would not break. This is a pretty accurate picture of the way Jesus conducted himself.

12:22-29

[22] *Then some people brought to Jesus a man who was blind and could not talk because he had a demon. Jesus healed the man, so that he was able to talk and see. [23] The crowds were all amazed. "Could he be the Son of David?" they asked.*

[24] *When the Pharisees heard this they replied, "He drives out demons only because their ruler Beelzebul gives him power to do so."*

[25] *Jesus knew what they were thinking and said to them, "Any country that divides itself into groups that fight each other will not last very long. And any town or family that divides itself into groups that fight each other will fall apart. [26] So if one group is fighting another in Satan's kingdom, this means that it is already divided into groups and will soon fall apart! [27] You say that I drive out demons because Beelzebul gives me the power to do so. Well, then, who gives your followers the power to drive them out? Your own followers prove that you are wrong! [28] No, it is God's Spirit who gives me the power to drive out demons, which proves that the Kingdom of God has already come upon you.*

[29] *"No one can break into a strong man's house and take away his belongings unless he ties up the strong man first; then he can plunder his house."*

Jesus' power over illness and over the forces of evil are the center of controversy here. The question at issue is not his power. The man blind and dumb could see and speak after Jesus healed him. There are two reactions. The crowd wonders whether he might be the messiah of God. But the Pharisees believe his action marks him as an agent of Beelzebul, one of the higher ranking members in the Kingdom of darkness.

Jesus in typical fashion responds by a proverb in verse 25. Then if anyone has failed to grasp the point he makes it explicit. If Satan is being undermined by a lower arch-fiend, then the Kingdom is collapsing from the inside.

Verse 27 points up that Jesus is not the only exorcist working in Israel. Jesus gives his opponents a lesson in logic when he indicates, that if he were casting out demons by the aid of Beelzebul, so must their own exorcists be judged. The honoring of exorcism within Judaism proves it is a godly activity.

The disease of the man was a disease of the spirit, which today would be characterized as psychosomatic. That is, it was a trouble in the man's soul which was physically manifested, much as there are certain ailments labeled hysterical in the present. By that is meant they have no clear organic cause.

Demon possession still occurs in the present. There are also still exorcists. The argument of Jesus is that his power over demons proves that he is against the devil and stronger than the devil.

12:30-32

[30] "Anyone who is not for me is really against me; anyone who does not help me gather is really scattering. [31] For this reason I tell you: men can be forgiven any sin and any evil thing they say; but whoever says evil things against the Holy Spirit will not be forgiven. [32] Anyone who says something against the Son of Man can be forgiven; but whoever says something against the Holy Spirit will not be forgiven — now or ever."

The fact that Jesus' appearance on earth is of crucial importance is again underlined in verse 30. God in the long haul does not allow for neutrality. People who think they can stand on the sidelines, while the future of the world — and of people's souls — is being determined, are deluded. One of the hardest lessons of life in this world is that it is not just a picnic. It is for keeps, and those who are not caught up in Jesus' mission are against him. Or to make it less personal, those who are not with him in the field gathering are scattering. There are no spectators in life.

One of the passages that causes people the most concern in the Bible is the saying of Jesus concerning the unforgivable sin — the sin against the Holy Spirit. Many are the persons who have understood themselves as cursed by God because they thought they had committed this sin.

It should be plainly said that the Bible does not state clearly what that sin is. The context, however, in which the saying is made concerns exorcism. Jesus says that people may be forgiven for speaking against him. As serious as it is to miss the centrality of Jesus in God's plans for the creation, it can be forgiven. But to speak against the Holy Spirit, that is something else.

The speaking against the Holy Spirit seems to have been the statement in verse 24 that Jesus' exorcisms were inspired by the devil. That was to suggest that God is not the author of goodness. But to separate goodness from "godness" is to confuse the moral order of the world. The Holy Spirit is the author of all good. And to attack goodness is to fall into a moral confusion from which there is no return.

12:33-37

[*33*] *"To have good fruit you must have a healthy tree; if you have a poor tree you will have bad fruit. For a tree is known by the kind of fruit it bears. [34] You snakes — how can you say good things when you are evil? For the mouth speaks what the heart is full of. [35] A good man brings good things out of his treasure of good things; a bad man brings bad things out of his treasure of bad things.*

[*36*] *"I tell you this: on the Judgment Day everyone will have to give account of every useless word he has ever spoken. [37] For your words will be used to judge you, either to declare you innocent or to declare you guilty."*

Jesus declared himself fully on the side of action over confession. He was markedly less concerned with words than with life. So it is that churches or confessions that emphasize right confession with less attention to life actions find themselves in tension with Jesus.

How a person acts reveals how he or she is in the heart.

Judgment Day will be a day of reckoning for everyone. Each person will be provided opportunity to speak before God's Tribunal in defense of his or her use of the power of speech, the power to reveal or deceive.

12:38-42

[38] Then some teachers of the Law and some Pharisees spoke up. "Teacher," they said, "we want to see you perform a miracle." [39] "How evil and godless are the people of this day!" Jesus exclaimed. "You ask me for a miracle? No! The only miracle you will be given is the miracle of the prophet Jonah. [40] In the same way that Jonah spent three days and nights in the belly of the big fish, so will the Son of Man spend three days and nights in the depths of the earth. [41] On the Judgment Day the people of Nineveh will stand up and accuse you, because they turned from their sins when they heard Jonah preach; and there is something here, I tell you, greater than Jonah! [42] On the Judgment Day the Queen from the South will stand up and accuse you, because she traveled halfway around the world to listen to Solomon's wise teaching; and there is something here, I tell you, greater than Solomon!"

Jesus was a wonder-worker who did not wish to do miracles as signs. He was quite willing to work wonders for human need, but not as demonstration of power or of his authority. In fact, the demand for a sign he understood as a sign of secularity. People were not willing to see the hand of God at work in ordinary life, and in the ministry he had conducted thus far. They wished the hand of God on demand — something that is not available to people in this world.

He rejects the demand for a sign. But he also says that a sign will be given in the course of his ministry, a sign as great as that of the prophet Jonah, who was swallowed by a big fish. The spectacular miracle of a man surviving three days inside a fish would be outdone by a man being raised from three days in the grave. The miracle would not be performed for the benefit of the curious. But it would be God's response to humanity's killing of Jesus.

The Jonah reference continues with a reference to his greatness and that of King Solomon. Yet Jesus was greater than either of these.

12:43-45

[43] "When an evil spirit goes out of a man, it travels over dry country looking for a place to rest. If it can't find one, [44] it says to itself, 'I will go back to my house which I left.' So it goes back and finds the house empty, clean, and all fixed up. [45] Then it goes out and brings along seven other spirits even worse than itself, and they come and live there. So that man is in worse shape, when it is all over, than he was at the beginning. This is the way it will happen to the evil people of this day."

Evil spirits constantly seek a home in the body. If they cannot dwell in a human, they prefer the bodies of animals. In some cases they are the evil souls of people who have not adjusted to their physical deaths. In others they are an order of spirits that have never been people.

The existence of such spirits means that a person can never be neutral in this world. If he or she is not a temple of the Holy Spirit, the person is vulnerable to demon possession.

In this saying the emphasis is on the necessity of one who has been exorcised to fill his or her life with the power of God, so that evil powers cannot return and retake possession.

12:46-50

[46] Jesus was still talking to the people when his mother and brothers arrived. They stood outside, asking to speak with him. [47] So one of the people there said to him, "Look, your mother and brothers are standing outside, and they want to speak with you."

[48] Jesus answered, "Who is my mother? Who are my brothers?" [49] Then he pointed to his disciples and said, "Look! Here are my mother and my brothers. [50] Whoever does what my Father in heaven wants him to do is my brother, my sister, my mother."

Jesus did not place an extraordinary emphasis upon family. He did love and care for them. One of his last thoughts was to make provision for his mother. Both Mary and his brother James were leaders in the Jerusalem church.

But he also refused to place blood above conduct. As an adult, people who stood close to him were any who did God's will, if even, presumably people that he did not know.

Matthew 13

13:1-9

[1] That same day Jesus left the house and went to the lakeside, where he sat down to teach. [2] The crowd that gathered around him was so large that he got into a boat and sat in it, while the crowd stood on the shore. [3] He used parables to tell them many things.

"There was a man who went out to sow. [4] As he scattered the seed in the field, some of it fell along the path, and the birds came and ate it up. [5] Some of it fell on rocky ground, where there was little soil. The seeds soon sprouted, because the soil wasn't deep. [6] When the sun came up it burned the young plants, and because the roots had not grown deep enough the plants soon dried up. [7] Some of the seed fell among thorns, which grew up and choked the plants. [8] But some seeds fell in good soil, and bore grain: some had one hundred grains, others sixty, and others thirty."

[9] And Jesus concluded, "Listen, then, if you have ears!"

Jesus did much of his teaching by parables. The modern western reader should remember that Jesus did not have a western education. He could not have taught as Paul by virtue of his Hebrew background. Thus one should not believe those who say Jesus taught in parables to be simple.

Further, parables are not simple. They are Jesus' way of trying to communicate heavenly things to earthly people. That is not easy under any circumstances. They are his attempt to communicate a deeper reality through word pictures.

Finally, parables are never exhausted. Any preacher knows that he can come back to a parable a year later and see richer meanings, exactly as can be done with a painting. Life is deepening the understanding of each person in a way that allows for a deeper perception of Jesus' meanings.

Recently a famous retired theologian said: "Now that I'm on nobody's payroll except Social Security's, I can admit to you that I don't understand the parables." What he meant was not that he had never been able to draw meaning from them, but that there were always depths there that he was unable to fathom. That is true because God is inexhaustible. And Jesus knew and was trying to communicate the mind of God.

The parable of the sower is a parable of growth. Even though much of the seed that is sown does not reach maturity because of problems or soil, enough does to assure a rich harvest. The point may simply be that God's word will enjoy a rich harvest.

Verse 9 assumes that an understanding heart must be present to perceive what it is Jesus is talking about.

13:10-17

[10] *Then the disciples came to Jesus and asked him, "Why do you use parables when you talk to them?"*

[11] *Jesus answered, "The knowledge of the secrets of the Kingdom of heaven has been given to you, but not to them.* [12] *For the man who has something will be given more, so that he will have more than enough; but the man who has nothing will have taken away from him even the little he has.* [13] *The reason that I use parables to talk to them is this: they look, but do not see, and they listen, but do not hear or understand.* [14] *So the prophecy of Isaiah comes true in their case:*
'You will listen and listen, but not understand;
you will look and look, but not see,
[15] *because this people's minds are dull,*
and they have stopped up their ears,
and have closed their eyes.
Otherwise, their eyes would see,
their ears would hear,
their minds would understand,
and they would turn to me, says God,
and I would heal them.'
[16] *"As for you, how fortunate you are! Your eyes see and your ears hear.* [17] *Remember this! Many prophets and many of God's people wanted very much to see what you see, but they could not, and to hear what you hear, but they did not."*

Perhaps the hardest saying in the New Testament is Jesus' answer when asked the purpose of parables. The plain meaning of the words is that Jesus has put his message into parable form to prevent people from understanding his meaning. It is interesting that Paul comes to the same conclusion about God's purposes in Romans 9-11. The fact that the bulk of the Jews rejected Jesus and his message is a part of the plan and purpose of God.

Matthew quotes an extended portion of Isaiah (6:9-10) which suggests that the people bear some responsibility for this situation. Further, it will not last forever. But for the time it is clear that the purpose is to conceal.

This is a hard saying because it is not customary to think of Jesus using strategies to conceal. Yet the same idea is there in Matthew, Mark, and Luke.

Verse 16 and following emphasize the blessedness of the disciples in having the opportunity to be at the center of God's revelation through Jesus.

13:18-23

[18] "Listen, then, and learn what the parable of the sower means. [19] Those who hear the message about the Kingdom but do not understand it are like the seed that fell along the path. The Evil One comes and snatches away what was sown in them. [20] The seed that fell on rocky ground stands for those who receive the message gladly as soon as they hear it. [21] But it does not sink deep in them, and they don't last long. So when trouble or persecution comes because of the message, they give up at once. [22] The seed fell among thorns stands for those who hear the message, but the worries about this life and the love for riches choke the message, and they don't bear fruit. [23] And the seed sown in the good soil stands for those who hear the message and understand it: they bear fruit, some as much as one hundred, others sixty, and others thirty."

This is a rare case where an interpretation of a parable is offered by Jesus. Some scholars have doubted that Jesus himself actually gave this interpretation, feeling that Jesus would not have offered an interpretation of his own parable. Those who so argue are strengthened by the fact that the interpretation does not occur at all in the Gospel of Thomas.

In any event it includes nothing that Jesus would not have said. And it is best to accept it, therefore, as part of the authentic voice of Jesus. The explanation is straightforward. The seed is the word of God. The various soils are varieties of people among whom the seed falls. The aim of the entire process is that the word would bear fruit.

13:24-30

[24] *Jesus told them another parable, "The Kingdom of heaven is like a man who sowed good seed in his field. [25] One night, when everyone was asleep, an enemy came and sowed weeds among the wheat, and went away. [26] When the plants grew and the heads of grain began to form, then the weeds showed up. [27] The man's servants came to him and said, 'Sir, it was good seed you sowed in your field; where did the weeds come from?' [28] 'It was some enemy who did this,' he answered. 'Do you want us to go and pull up the weeds?' they asked him. [29] 'No,' he answered, 'because as you gather the weeds you might pull up some of the wheat along with them. [30] Let the wheat and the weeds both grow together until harvest, and then I will tell the harvest workers: 'Pull up the weeds first and tie them in bundles to throw in the fire; then gather in the wheat and put it in my barn.' "*

This parable, unlike previous ones, introduces itself as an attempt to describe what the Kingdom of God (the realm where things are as God intends) is like. In this case one of the profound mysteries of the world is dealt with in story form. The question addressed is: why does the world consist of a mixture of good and evil? More than one philosopher has long pondered this question, as well as a host of ordinary people confronted with suffering.

Jesus does not offer all the answers, but the following points are clear in the parable. The field is the world. The seed sown is that (or, those people) which makes for good in the world. An enemy, who is no further identified than that, sows evil. When the deed is discovered the man commands that the bad be allowed to remain so that the good are not accidently uprooted. At the harvest the evil are destroyed and the good are gathered into the man's barns.

Many questions are not answered. But the direction is clear. However mixed the world may be at present — the evil does not come from the planter but an enemy. And evil will be destroyed in the end but the good will triumph.

In such a way did Jesus express his philosophy.

13:31-32

[31] *Jesus told them another parable, "The Kingdom of heaven is like*

a mustard seed, which a man takes and sows in his field. [32] It is the smallest of all seeds, but when it grows up it is the biggest of all plants. It becomes a tree, so that the birds come and make their nests in its branches."

This is one of the shorter parables. The Kingdom is very small in the present. But when it has completed its growth it will dwarf everything. This parable is a source of comfort to those who have sung "and though the wrong seems oft so strong, God is the ruler yet."

Power alone is not God-like, but power in the service of the good. Thus the final image of the mustard plant is of a growth that provides shelter and shade for the birds of the area.

13:33

[33] Jesus told them another parable, "The Kingdom of heaven is like yeast. A woman takes it and mixes it with a bushel of flour, until the whole batch of dough rises."

This is one of those parables where one is reminded that most people are reading the saying of Jesus in its third language. Jesus taught in Aramaic (or possibly Hebrew). This was translated into Greek. And modern Christians know the saying in yet another translation, in this case, English.

The word translated in this text "mix" is in Greek **enkruptein,** which is most naturally translated "hide in." It would then read: "A woman takes it and hides it in a bushel of flour."

In any translation the power of the Kingdom of God to transform the entire world is clearly expressed in the parable. If, in addition, the woman hid the leaven (yeast) in the flour, she must have been surprised indeed at the spectacular growth of a bushel of flour raised. That translation includes a picture of humor, surprise, and irrepressibility.

13:34-35

[34] Jesus used parables to tell all these things to the crowds; he would not say a thing to them without using a parable. [35] He did this to make come true what the prophet had said,

"I will use parables when I speak to them;
I will tell them things unknown since the creation of the world."

Earlier the emphasis was upon the quality of a parable to keep people in the dark. Here Matthew cites Psalms 78:2 to indicate the parable as a method of revealing, as a way of translating the profundity of God to the crowds that gathered to hear him.

13:36-43

[36] *Then Jesus left the crowd and went indoors. His disciples came to him and said, "Tell us what the parable of the weeds in the field means."*

[37] *Jesus answered, "The man who sowed the good seed is the Son of Man;* [38] *the field is the world; the good seed is the people who belong to the Kingdom; the weeds are the people who belong to the Evil One;* [39] *and the enemy who sowed the weeds is the Devil. The harvest is the end of the age, and the harvest workers are angels.* [40] *Just as the weeds are gathered up and burned in the fire, so it will be at the end of the age:* [41] *the Son of Man will send out his angels and they will gather up out of his Kingdom all who cause people to sin, and all other evildoers,* [42] *and throw them into the fiery furnace, where they will cry and gnash their teeth.* [43] *Then God's people will shine like the sun in their Father's Kingdom. Listen, then, if you have ears!"*

The parable of the tares is also offered as an interpretation by Jesus privately to his disciples. It is roughly the interpretation that was given earlier, except that the Son of Man is seen as the sower. The use of the angels as harvesters is also a detail one would not naturally draw from the parable. Yet the angels are certainly available to do God's bidding.

This is a clear text for the punishment of the wicked, first those who lead others astray and then all sorts of evildoers. It does not necessarily teach eternal punishment but it does teach punishment after death for some. Anyone who rejects such a notion has strayed far from biblical religion indeed.

13:44

[44] *"The Kingdom of heaven is like a treasure hidden in a field. A man happens to find it, so he covers it up again. He is so happy that he goes and sells everything he has, and then goes back and buys the field."*

Jesus' sayings approach the description of the Kingdom of God from many different angles. No one saying exhausts it, any more than one theologian can exhaust God's meaning. Here the emphasis is upon the supreme importance of the Kingdom. Without hesitation, a sensible man will happily part with everything he has to have it.

13:45-46

[45] *"Also, the Kingdom of heaven is like a buyer looking for fine pearls. [46] When he finds one that is unusually fine, he goes and sells everything he has, and buys the pearl."*

The parable of the pearl buyer is similar to the parable of the field, except that in this parable the Kingdom is compared to a pearl. Nor is it an ordinary pearl, but one that would bring a pearl merchant to dispose of all of his other pearls in order to obtain.

13:47-50

[47] *"Also, the Kingdom of heaven is like a net thrown out in the lake, which catches all kinds of fish. [48] When it is full, the fishermen pull it to shore and sit down to divide the fish: the good ones go into their buckets, the worthless ones are thrown away. [49] It will be like this at the end of the age: the angels will go out and gather up the evil people from among the good, [50] and throw them into the fiery furnace. There they will cry and gnash their teeth."*

The Kingdom is not always presented in its beauty. It also includes elements of judgment. In this case the comparison is to fishing, certainly a clear picture to a community of disciples which included at least four fisherman. The comparison is between edible and inedible fish. The edible are kept and the rest are thrown away.

This parable clearly demonstrates that this is a word picture and not an exact comparison. No human being would consider it a privilege to be a good fish that is eaten. Rather, the comparison is more general. There is judgment. The evil people will be consigned to punishment (a fiery furnace). Nothing is described as happening to the good people. Of course, if the bad are removed, that would probably be sufficient to make this world heavenly.

13:51-52

[51] "Do you understand these things?" Jesus asked them. "Yes," they answered.

[52] So he replied, "This means, then, that every teacher of the Law who becomes a disciple in the Kingdom of heaven is like a homeowner who takes new and old things out of his storage room."

The clearest indication that Jesus did not intend a rejection of his native Judaism is found in this little saying. He was not the bringer of a new religion. And he did not understand his disciples so to be. The model he sets forth for every disciple is that of one who has the knack to combine the old and the new.

This means that a Christianity that disdains Judaism or the Old Testament is a warped Christianity. To the Jews belongs the promise. Likewise a religious movement that focuses simply on the present has lost its ability to draw from the riches of the past. And a movement centered on the past cannot appreciate what God is doing in the present.

Jesus wanted the two together.

13:53-58

[53] When Jesus finished telling these parables, he left that place [54] and went back to his home town. He taught in their synagogue, and those who heard him were amazed. "Where did he get such wisdom?" they asked. "And what about his miracles? [55] Isn't he the carpenter's son? Isn't Mary his mother, and aren't James, Joseph, Simon, and Judas his brothers? [56] Aren't all his sisters living here? Where did he get all this?" [57] And so they rejected him.

Jesus said to them, "A prophet is respected everywhere except in his home town and by his own family." [58] He did not perform many miracles there because they did not have faith.

Another example of the reliability of the Gospels is found in the account of Jesus' reception in his home town. Earlier it has been indicated that sometime in his adult life Jesus had moved from Nazareth to Capernaum. He had likely been gone for some time.

When he returned, the people were not prepared for who he became. Jesus as preacher and miracle worker was not what they had been led to expect from knowing him as the son of a local family. Further, his mother, his brothers, and his sisters did not presage such a person.

They could not accept the fact that something great could come from among them. Rather than to think so highly of themselves and their town, they rejected him.

Apparently Mary and Joseph has said nothing about the virgin birth. Such knowledge must have prepared Mary and Joseph to expect the unusual from Jesus. Nothing is known of Joseph when Jesus reached adulthood.

Jesus' response that a prophet is acknowledged everywhere but by his townsfolk and family point up the fact that Jesus' conduct also disturbed his family. It is also known however, that later both his Mother and James became a part of his ministry.

Verse 58 acknowledges that Jesus did not do many wonders there because the people did not believe in him. Mark makes it even more clear that he was prevented from doing wonders there because of their lack of faith.

94

Matthew 14

Matthew 14:1-12

[1] It was at that time that Herod, the ruler of Galilee, heard about Jesus. [2] "He is really John the Baptist, who has come back to life," he told his officials. "That is why these powers are at work in him."

[3] For Herod had ordered John's arrest, and had him tied up and put in prison. He did this because of Herodias, his brother Philip's wife. [4] John the Baptist kept telling Herod, "It isn't right for you to marry her!" [5] Herod wanted to kill him, but he was afraid of the Jewish people, because they considered John to be a prophet.

[6] On Herod's birthday the daughter of Herodias danced in front of the whole group. Herod was so pleased [7] that he promised her, "I swear that I will give you anything you ask for!"

[8] At her mother's suggestion she asked him, "Give me right here the head of John the Baptist on a plate!"

[9] The king was sad, but because of the promise he had made in front of all his guests he gave orders that her wish be granted. [10] So he had John beheaded in prison. [11] The head was brought in on a plate and given to the girl, who took it to her mother. [12] John's disciples came, got his body, and buried it; then they went and told Jesus.

The family of Herod was a troubled group. Wealth and power do not satisfy with peace of mind. And the Herods were troubled. Herod Antipas had taken the wife of his brother. (Ancient historical references indicate differences on who was married to whom.) John, who did not distinguish between private religion and public morality, would give Herod no peace on this issue.

John must have made an impression upon Herod's soul, because even after John was dead, Herod suspected that Jesus was merely John returned to haunt him.

Herod had killed John at the urging of the daughter of Herodias, Salome. Literature has made much of this dance, and it must have been impressive to so move Herod. But in fact there is no description of the girl, her clothing or lack of it, or the dance. The rest has been added by fertile imaginations.

14:13-21

[13] When Jesus heard the news, he left that place in a boat and went to a lonely place by himself. The people heard about it, left their towns, and followed him by land. [14] Jesus got out of the boat, and when he saw

the large crowd his heart was filled with pity for them, and he healed their sick.

[15] That evening his disciples came to him and said, "It is already very late, and this is a lonely place. Send the people away and let them go to the villages and buy food for themselves."

[16] "They don't have to leave," answered Jesus. "You yourselves give them something to eat."

[17] "All we have here are five loaves and two fish," they replied.

[18] "Bring them here to me," Jesus said. [19] He ordered the people to sit down on the grass; then he took the five loaves and the two fish, looked up to heaven, and gave thanks to God. He broke the loaves and gave them to the disciples, and the disciples gave them to the people. [20] Everyone ate and had enough. Then the disciples took up twelve baskets full of what was left over. [21] The number of men who ate was about five thousand, not counting the women and children.

The death of John was a great blow to Jesus. He had earlier said that no one born of woman was greater than John. Although their personal styles were quite different, he saw in John a soul mate on the issue of the central importance of the will of God.

Further, the death of John must have foreshadowed for Jesus his own death. A person who lived totally focused upon the will of God without concern for personal safety might expect to wear the martyr's crown.

But Jesus was not long left to his thoughts and prayers. Human need soon surrounded him. The disciples responded with compassion when they saw that the crowd around Jesus had been so long without food. Jesus shared their compasson but had a marvelous solution.

The feeding of the 5,000 is one of the genuinely mysterious wonders that Jesus performed. Some look at it and say that he multiplied the loaves and fishes. Certainly Jesus had that power — as Satan had known in the temptation story. Some say that the crowd had brought food and the example of sharing moved them to share what they had. If that is where the food came from, then it was a miracle of the human spirit.

14:22-33

[22] Then Jesus made the disciples get into the boat and go ahead of him to the other side of the lake, while he sent the people away. [23]

After sending the people away, he went up a hill by himself to pray. When evening came, Jesus was there alone; [24] by this time the boat was far out in the lake, tossed about by the waves, because the wind was blowing against it. [25] Between three and six o'clock in the morning Jesus came to them, walking on the water [26] When the disciples saw him walking on the water they were terrified. "It's a ghost!" they said, and screamed with fear.

[27] Jesus spoke to them at once. "Courage!" he said. "It is I. Don't be afraid!"

[28] Then Peter spoke up. "Lord," he said, "if it is really you, order me to come out on the water to you."

[29] "Come!" answered Jesus. So Peter got out of the boat and started walking on the water to Jesus. [30] When he noticed the wind, however, he was afraid, and started to sink down in the water. "Save me, Lord!" he cried.

[31] At once Jesus reached out and grabbed him and said, "How little faith you have! Why did you doubt?"

[32] They both got into the boat, and the wind died down. [33] The disciples in the boat worshiped Jesus. "Truly you are the Son of God!" they exclaimed.

People are always frightened of ghosts. They appear suddenly, are only partially visible, and signify the intrusion of another dimension into ordinary earthly existence. The incident of Jesus' walking on the water struck the disciples like that.

The event must have been quite different to Jesus. He came perhaps to be of assistance because the disciples were making so little headway against the wind. He does not seem to have thought about it one way or another. Was he surprised when he took his first step on the lake to find that the water supported him? Or did he expect it?

Only Matthew tells the extra incident of Peter walking on the water. One of Peter's best characteristics was his confidence that he could do anything his Lord could do. He often failed, of course. But sometimes he succeeded. And he would have had no success if he had not tried.

When Peter began to sink, it was because he feared. Fear is the opposite of faith. Faith goes forward and fear shrinks back.

At the point at which Peter and Jesus entered the boat, the wind dropped. It was in response to this cooperation of nature with Jesus that the disciples worshiped him as Son of God.

14:34-36

[34] They crossed the lake and came to land at Gennesaret, [35] where the people recognized Jesus. So they sent for the sick people in all the surrounding country and brought them to Jesus. [36] They begged him to let the sick at least touch the edge of his cloak; and all who touched it were made well.

Jesus gained in popularity because of his healing powers. At Gennesaret the spectacular nature of his ability was demonstrated when people could be healed simply by touching his garment.

Matthew 15

Matthew 15:1-9

[1] *Then some Pharisees and teachers of the Law came to Jesus from Jerusalem and asked him,* [2] *"Why is it that your disciples disobey the teaching handed down by our ancestors? They don't wash their hands in the proper way before they eat!"*

[3] *Jesus answered, "And why do you disobey God's command and follow your own teaching?* [4] *For God said 'Honor your father and mother,' and 'Anyone who says bad things about his father or mother must be put to death.'* [5] *But you teach that if a person has something he could use to help his father or mother, but says, 'This belongs to God,'* [6] *he does not need to honor his father. This is how you disregard God's word to follow your own teaching.* [7] *You hypocrites! How right Isaiah was when he prophesied about you!*

[8] *'These people, says God, honor me with their words,*
but their heart is really far away from me.
[9] *It is no use for them to worship me,*
because they teach man-made commandments as though they were God's rules!'"

There were at least two positions represented toward the Law of Moses in Jesus' time. The Sadducees taught that the people were bound to observe only the written Law of Moses. The Pharisees believed that Moses had also passed down oral law, equally important as the written law. The oral law, which was argued, discussed, and interpreted by various rabbis, eventually was written in the Mishna, sometime after Jesus.

Jesus was closer to the Sadducees than the Pharisees on this point, in that he does not seem to credit oral law. (In many other beliefs, such as the reality of angels and the resurrection of the dead, he was closer to the Pharisees.)

Jesus further distinguished what he regarded as the more important moral/ethical (as distinct from the ceremonial) elements of the law. In this case, he responds to the Pharisees in such a way as to suggest their concern for clean hands is petty by comparison to their encouragement of the neglect of parents by urging the assignment of property to God. Jesus has no doubt that God is more concerned with carrying out obligations to family than with gifts of money or gifts to God. Many people today are misled by radio evangelists or cultic groups into contributions, often to the neglect of their families and the fattening of the savings accounts of evangelistic organizations. Jesus did not appreciate that teaching.

Again Isaiah (29:13) is quoted on the side of those who do not follow unwritten laws.

15:10-20

[10] Then Jesus called the crowd to him and said to them, "Listen; and understand! [11] It is not what goes into a person's mouth that makes him unclean; rather, what comes out of it makes him unclean."

[12] Then the disciples came to him and said, "Do you know that the Pharisees had their feelings hurt by what you said?"

[13] "Every plant which my Father in heaven did not plant will be pulled up," answered Jesus. [14] "Don't worry about them! They are blind leaders; and when one blind man leads another one, both fall into a ditch."

[15] Peter spoke up, "Tell us what this parable means."

[16] Jesus said to them, "You are still no more intelligent than the others. [17] Don't you understand? Anything that goes into a person's mouth goes into his stomach and then on out of the body. [18] But the things that come out of the mouth come from the heart; such things make a man unclean. [19] For from his heart come the evil ideas which lead him to kill, commit adultery, and do other immoral things; to rob, lie, and slander others. [20] These are the things that make a man unclean. But to eat without washing your hands as they say you should — this does not make a man unclean."

Jesus demonstrated that he was also concerned about cleanliness, but it was not a concern for ritual cleanliness, not for what goes into the mouth but for what comes out of the mouth. Jesus was quite convinced that the mouth was a direct link to the heart, and that sooner or later the mouth would reveal the purity or impurity of a person. Modern psychology has made much the same discovery regarding people, that is, a trained hearer can discern the values of people through clues in conversation patterns.

Jesus was also straightforward about what makes a person unclean. It is murder, adultery, immorality, robbery, lies, and slander. These are all sins against neighbor. In the face of such human activity, Jesus could not care less about the question of cleaning hands before eating. He would not have agreed with the proverb, "Cleanliness is next to godliness."

Verse 12 reveals the natural concern about the Pharisees considering the strong position Jesus took regarding ritual cleanliness. Christians today are still a bit embarrassed with their Jewish friends concerning these strong positions. The Pharisees were being loyal to many concerns for ritual cleanliness found in the Old Testament. Neither all ancient Jews nor all modern Jews should be regarded as seeking to distort God's will. They were trying to honor it as they understood it.

But Jesus had no patience with niceties. In this he was one with John the Baptizer. He was for what God wanted. And he did not want to say anything to suggest that the Pharisees were legitimate teachers of the people.

15:21-28

[21] *Jesus left that place and went off to the territory near the cities of Tyre and Sidon.* [22] *A Canaanite woman who lived in that region came to him. "Son of David, sir!" she cried. "Have mercy on me! My daughter has a demon and is in a terrible condition."*

[23] *But Jesus did not say a word to her. His disciples came to him and begged him, "Send her away! She is following us and making all this noise!"*

[24] *Then Jesus replied, "I have been sent only to the lost sheep of the people of Israel."*

[25] *At this the woman came and fell at his feet. "Help me, sir!" she said.*

[26] *Jesus answered, "It isn't right to take the children's food and throw it to the dogs."*

[27] *"That is true, sir," she answered; "but even the dogs eat the leftovers that fall from their masters' table."*

[28] *So Jesus answered her, "You are a woman of great faith! What you want will be done for you." And at that very moment her daughter was healed.*

There is no more important text to demonstrate that faith is more important than religion. Every religion has its doctrines, rules, and regulations. And these are important to the members of that religious group. Jesus, too, acknowledged the religion into which he was born.

When he was approached by a Gentile woman, he responded that his mission was to Israel only.

It is not surprising that Jesus would understand his mission as thus limited. The Jews had been God's chosen people since Abraham. The Messiah (Anointed) was the Anointed of Israel. What is surprising is that, in the face of the woman's persistence on behalf of her child, Jesus changed his mind. One must look hard in the Gospels to find examples of Jesus changing his thinking.

But on this occasion he learned something from a persistent woman.

15:29-31

[29] *Jesus left that place and went along by Lake Galilee. He climbed a hill and sat down. [30] Large crowds came to him, bringing with them the lame, the blind, the crippled, the dumb, and many other sick people, whom they placed at Jesus' feet; and he healed them. [31] The people were amazed as they saw the dumb speaking, the crippled whole, the lame walking, and the blind seeing; and they praised the God of Israel.*

It is truly amazing how much of Jesus' ministry was given over to healing. How many were the lives and bodies renewed because he had passed among people of that day. There have been healers in many generations. But such a healer as Jesus came along only once. And people knew that the blessing of God was on him!

15:32-39

[32] *Jesus called his disciples to him and said, "I feel sorry for these people, because they have been with me for three days and now have nothing to eat. I don't want to send them away without feeding them, because they might faint on their way home."*

[33] *The disciples asked him, "Where will we find enough food in this desert to feed this crowd?"*

[34] *"How much bread do you have?" Jesus asked.*

"Seven loaves," they answered, "and a few small fish."

[35] *So Jesus ordered the crowd to sit down on the ground. [36] Then he took the seven loaves and the fish, gave thanks to God, broke them and gave them to the disciples, and the disciples gave them to the people. [37] They all ate and had enough. The disciples took up seven baskets full of pieces left over. [38] The number of men who ate was four thousand, not counting the women and children.*

[39] *Then Jesus sent the people away, got into the boat, and went to the territory of Magadan.*

This story provides an opportunity to discuss gospel transmission. Between the ministry of Jesus and the formation of the written Gospels there is a period of anywhere from twenty to forty years. In that time the sayings and stories were collected, translated, and eventually organized into Gospels by the evangelists.

Some scholars have argued that, in the above story, one has a duplicate of the story of the feeding of the 5,000, passing along in separate sources so that the evangelist, upon finding it, thought them to be separate stories. The contents are roughly the same as the feeding of the 5,000.

Matthew 16

Matthew 16:1-4

[1] *Some Pharisees and Sadducees came to Jesus. They wanted to trap him, so they asked him to perform a miracle for them, to show God's approval.* [2] *But Jesus answered, "When the sun is setting you say, 'We are going to have fine weather, because the sky is red.' [3] And early in the morning you say, 'It is going to rain, because the sky is red and dark.' You can predict the weather by looking at the sky; but you cannot interpret the signs concerning these times! [4] How evil and godless are the people of this day! You ask me for a miracle? No! The only miracle you will be given is the miracle of Jonah."*

So he left them and went away.

Jesus is consistent in refusing to present a miracle on demand. He criticizes his generation for the contrast between their ability to read natural signs and their blindness concerning divine patterns at work in the world. If that is a valid criticism of the ancient world, it is triply true for modern times. Technology has made great strides and weather patterns can be studied from satellite pictures. But people are not any wiser in discerning the hand of God in human events. Many would deny it entirely.

Again the only sign to be forthcoming is the sign of Jonah.

16:5-12

[5] *When the disciples crossed over to the other side of the lake, they forgot to take any bread.* [6] *Jesus said to them, "Look out, and be on your guard against the yeast of the Pharisees and Sadducees."*

[7] *They started discussing among themselves, "He says this because we didn't bring any bread."*

[8] *Jesus knew what they were saying, so he asked them, "Why are you discussing among yourselves about not having any bread? How little faith you have! [9] Don't you understand yet? Don't you remember when I broke the five loaves for the five thousand men? How many baskets did you fill? [10] And what about the seven loaves for the four thousand men? How many baskets did you fill? [11] How is it that you don't understand that I was not talking to you about bread? Guard yourselves from the yeast of the Pharisees and Sadducees!"*

[12] *Then the disciples understood that he was not telling them to guard themselves from the yeast used in bread, but from the teaching of the Pharisees and Sadducees.*

This extended section highlights the difficulty that the disciples had in understanding Jesus. A popular theme in recent years has been to view the ignorance of the disciples more as a literary device of the evangelist than as an historical reality. Yet to be with Jesus must have been a mind-boggling experience. Jesus would have been difficult for anyone to understand.

In this story Jesus speaks of leaven as a metaphor. He warned the disciples not to involve themselves in the teaching of either of the two major competing groups to Jesus' own teaching.

16:13-20

[13] *Jesus went to the territory near the town of Caesarea Philippi, where he asked his disciples, "Who do men say the Son of Man is?"*

[14] *"Some say John the Baptist," they answered. "Others say Elijah, while others say Jeremiah or some other prophet."*

[15] *"What about you?" he asked them. "Who do you say I am?"*

[16] *Simon Peter answered, "You are the Messiah, the Son of the living God."*

[17] *"Good for you, Simon, son of John!" answered Jesus. "Because this truth did not come to you from any human being, but it was given to you directly by my Father in heaven. [18] And so I tell you: you are a rock, Peter and on this rock foundation I will build my church, which not even death will ever be able to overcome. [19] I will give you the keys of the Kingdom of heaven; what you prohibit on earth will be prohibited in heaven; what you permit on earth will be permitted in heaven."*

[20] *Then Jesus ordered his disciples not to tell anyone that he was the Messiah.*

This passage is generally regarded as the turning point in the ministry of Jesus. Up to this point Jesus has been protective about his own identity. He has hidden his purposes from outsiders and even to an extent from his own disciples. It is as if he wished them to draw their own conclusions.

Then at Caesarea Philippi, a lovely mountain spot well to the north of the Sea of Galilee, he put it to his own disciples. Two questions: Who do people take me to be? Who do you take me to be?

The answers to the first were John the Baptizer, Elijah, Jeremiah, or some other prophet. John the Baptizer has been mentioned already as Herod's guess.

John had made a major impact, and it is not surprising that his name would be close to people's lips. Elijah is the Old Testament character who performed miracles like Jesus, including raising people from the dead. Those who thought Jesus was Jeremiah or another prophet saw in Jesus' clear teaching of God's word the character and obedience of a prophet.

Jesus was also interested in hearing from the disciples. The very first person who spoke hit paydirt, according the Matthew's version of this story. When Peter called Jesus Messiah, Jesus responded by saying that Peter's answer was a sign of God's blessing. This sign Jesus took as occasion to name Peter as head of his church, with the same power to forgive and bind as Jesus himself commanded.

These are the only two examples of the word church [ecclesia] in the Gospels.

16:21-28

[21] *From that time on Jesus began to say plainly to his disciples, "I must go to Jerusalem and suffer much from the elders, the chief priests, and the teachers of the Law. I will be put to death, and on the third day I will be raised to life."*

[22] *Peter took him aside and began to rebuke him. "God forbid it, Lord!" he said. "This must never happen to you!"*

[23] *Jesus turned around and said to Peter, "Get away from me, Satan! You are an obstacle in my way, because these thoughts of yours are men's thoughts, not God's!"*

[24] *Then Jesus said to his disciples, "If anyone wants to come with me, he must forget himself, carry his cross, and follow me. [25] For whoever wants to save his own life will lose it; but whoever loses his life for my sake will find it. [26] Will a man gain anything if he wins the whole world but loses his life? Of course not! There is nothing a man can give to regain his life. [27] For the son of Man is about to come in the glory of his Father with his angels, and then he will repay everyone according to his deeds. [28] Remember this! There are some here who will not die until they have seen the Son of Man come as King."*

The elevation of Peter to eventual headship of the church did not protect him from serious error. When Jesus announced to his disciples that mission included a death in Jerusalem, Peter objected strenuously.

It is true that he objected because of his love for

Jesus. He was not even thinking ahead to the personal
danger there might be for him. He wanted to protect the
greatest force for good he had ever encountered. What
a waste for Jesus to die.

Jesus' sharp response, calling Peter Satan, shows
what a serious temptation Peter's suggestion was for
Jesus. Jesus was normal enough not to want to die, to
use his power for the improvement of life in the world.
But he also knew he should not dwell on that side of
things. Those temptations had been offered earlier by
Satan and he had no need to return to them again.

One advantage of Peter's outburst was that it drew
from Jesus a statement of God's view of life. The victory
goes to the one who gives up all. Gaining the entire world
is to no advantage for it cannot be kept. The meaning of
life is in cross-bearing, in following the path of Jesus.

Verse 28 presents Jesus' prediction that some of his
hearers would be alive when the Son of Man comes as
King. At least two possibilities present themselves here.
Jesus could have reference to his resurrection, at which
point God declared him King. But that does not mean a
coming as King. It could be a general reference to what
happened in the outpouring of the Holy Spirit at
Pentecost. Or it could be a reference to the coming in
judgment which, as it is normally understood, has not
yet happened. Since Jesus says elsewhere that only God
knows that time, perhaps he expected that it would be
much sooner than it turned out to be.

Matthew 17

Matthew 17:1-5

[1] Six days later Jesus took with him Peter and the brothers James and John, and led them up a high mountain by themselves. [2] As they looked on, a change came over him: his face became as bright as the sun, and his clothes as white as light. [3] Then the three disciples saw Moses and Elijah talking with Jesus. [4] So Peter spoke up and said to Jesus, "Lord, it is a good thing that we are here; if you wish, I will make three tents here, one for you, one for Moses, and one for Elijah."

[5] While he was talking, a shining cloud came over them and a voice said from the cloud: "This is my own dear Son, with whom I am well pleased — listen to him!"

Three of Jesus' disciples saw the Son of Man as King only six days later. It may well be that this was the event to which Jesus referred in verse 28.

The appearance of Jesus transfigured with two biblical figures in whose steps he walked was an awesome event. The description sounds as if Moses and Elijah did not fully materialize, in the fashion of Jesus' post-resurrection body so that he could even eat. Rather it seems as if Jesus was translated into another dimension so that he might converse with them. It is a dimension characterized by light, as is normally true of the appearances of angels.

The disciples — Peter, James, and John — were able to see the conversation, and their response was the same as the patriarchs before them. They wished to make a sanctuary there.

God appeared also, by voice, through a shining cloud as in Exodus, and said the same thing he had said at Jesus' baptism. The fact that God speaks up here strengthens the idea that this is the beginning of the second stage of Jesus' mission.

17:6-13

[6] When the disciples heard the voice they were so terrified that they threw themselves face down to the ground. [7] Jesus came to them and touched them. "Get up," he said. "Don't be afraid!" [8] So they looked up and saw no one else except Jesus.

[9] As they came down the mountain Jesus ordered them, "Don't tell

108

anyone about this vision you have seen until the Son of Man has been raised from death."

[10] Then the disciples asked Jesus, "Why do the teachers of the Law say that Elijah has to come first?"

[11] "Elijah does indeed come first," answered Jesus, "and he will get everything ready. [12] But I tell you this: Elijah has already come and people did not recognize him, but treated him just as they pleased. In the same way the Son of Man will also be mistreated by them."

[13] Then the disciples understood that he was talking to them about John the Baptist.

The terror at the voice of God is a stronger reaction than is normal to a heavenly voice. It is quite normal that people are frightened by such an event. In this case it seems that the stronger reaction is brought about by the fact that the limits of the three disciples' confidence had already been tested to the limit of the transfiguration of Jesus and the appearance with him of Moses and Elijah. The addition of God's voice was enough to drive them to distraction. They were no doubt relieved when Jesus had returned to his normal appearance and was fully present in this dimension again.

Jesus' command that the disciples not share this story until after his resurrection was perhaps motivated by people's inability to comprehend it.

The appearance of Elijah at Jesus' transfiguration prompted the disciples to ask concerning the expectation that an appearance of Elijah would signal the Day of the Lord (Malachi 4:5). The answer of Jesus convinces the disciples that John the Baptizer was Elijah.

What does it mean that John the Baptizer was Elijah? Some take it as evidence that Jesus believed in reincarnation. Certainly the plain meaning of verse 12 is that Elijah has come again. Such a passage is a weak foundation for reincarnation, however, in that what may be said for a special leader of the people (who did not die but was taken into heaven by a whirlwind, 2 Kings 2:11) does not necessarily apply to every person. Further, the general pattern of Jesus' speech is in the direction of metaphor, that is John was the Elijah that was expected. Still, it is a mysterious saying. The focus is upon the mistreatment of John and the corresponding coming mistreatment of Jesus.

17:14-21

[14] When they returned to the crowd, a man came to Jesus, knelt before him, [15] and said, "Sir, have mercy on my son! He is epileptic and has such terrible fits that he often falls in the fire or in the water. [16] I brought him to your disciples, but they could not heal him."

[17] Jesus answered, "How unbelieving and wrong you people are! How long must I stay with you? How long do I have to put up with you? Bring the boy here to me!" [18] Jesus commanded the demon and it went out, so that the boy was healed at that very moment.

[19] Then the disciples came to Jesus in private and asked him, "Why couldn't we drive the demon out?"

[20] "It was because you do not have enough faith," answered Jesus. "Remember this! If you have faith as big as a mustard seed, you can say to this hill, 'Go from here to there!' and it will go. You could do anything! [21] (But only prayer and fasting can drive this kind out; nothing else can.)"

The use of the word epileptic in this translation is misleading. Mark's and Luke's parallel texts both refer to a spirit as the cause of this condition. Jesus in Matthew actually says that the boy is moon stricken. It would be irresponsible to assume because the translator has chosen to use the word 'epileptic' that epileptics are automatically victims of demon possession. Modern medicine and psychology have added richly to the description of disease and the multiple causes of it. Demons do still beset people, but they are only one cause. Jesus has power over all illness, including one that physicians still cannot handle with knife or chemistry, that is, death.

The issue at stake in this story is the inability of the disciples to heal the boy. Jesus reprimanded them for their lack of faith, and drove the demon out.

The entire incident prompted Jesus to discourse on the power of faith. In one of his more striking sayings, he says, "If you had faith as a mustard seed." The translator thinks that Jesus was talking about the size of a mustard seed. That is impossible. Perhaps, however, he was talking about the ability of this tiny seed to break the earth, to grow up to take its place among the larger plants. That kind of faith is able to move hills and mountains. The saying underlines faith as the strongest force humans have available to them because it forges a direct link to the power of God, who built the hills in the first place.

Verse 21 is in brackets because it may not have been a part of the original text. In many early manuscripts it is not. In many it is. In either case, it refers to the power of fasting to heighten the spiritual concentration required for prayer.

17:22-23

[22] *When the disciples all came together in Galilee, Jesus said to them, "The Son of Man is about to be handed over to men [23] who will kill him; but on the third day he will be raised to life."*

The disciples became very sad.

Jesus repeated his new message about his coming death and resurrection. The disciples, who had to this point focused on his success, and their own, as healers, as well as his popularity as a teacher, did not understand why there was any need for a death. It was they who were concerned that he should not unnecessarily aggravate the religious leaders. Now he said again that his mission included suffering and death.

17:24-27

[24] *When Jesus and his disciples came to Capernaum, the collectors of the temple tax came to Peter and asked, "Does your teacher pay the temple tax?"*

[25] *"Of course," Peter answered.*

When Peter went into the house, Jesus spoke up first, "Simon, what is your opinion? Who pays duties or taxes to the kings of this world? The citizens of the country or the foreigners?"

[26] *"The foreigners," answered Peter.*

"Well, then," replied Jesus, "that means that the citizens don't have to pay. [27] But we don't want to offend these people. So go to the lake and drop in a line; pull up the first fish you hook, and in its mouth you will find a coin worth enough for my temple tax and yours; take it and pay them our taxes."

Some passages in the Bible are easy to understand. Some are difficult because of their spiritual depth. Some are difficult because of the differences in customs between the ancient world and the modern. This story is difficult because of a difference in custom.

The key question is asked by Jesus: "Who pays duties or taxes to the kings of this world? The citizens of the country or the foreigners (sons of the king)?" The answer modern people, accustomed to shelling out large amounts for tax even before they see their paycheck, expect is citizens. But in the ancient world the advantage of being a citizen was that one was not taxed. Taxes were raised for the Roman Empire from the provinces and the vassal states. Certainly citizens did not pay.

Jesus argued from this common practice that he and Peter did not have to pay the temple tax, since they were sons of the King (God). This is a wonderful story for those who are burdened because they feel Christianity lays so many obligations upon them. They are not obligated. They are sons of the King with Peter and Jesus.

Almost an epilog to the story is the fact that Jesus found an ingenious means to pay the temple tax: his stated reason, not to be offensive. It seems that he was willing to pay his share if it was not laid on as an obligation. He was willing to contest with religious authority, but he did not on this issue.

Matthew 18

Matthew 18:1-5

[1] *At that moment the disciples came to Jesus, asking, "Who is the greatest in the Kingdom of heaven?"*
[2] *Jesus called a child, had him stand in front of them,* [3] *and said, "Remember this! Unless you change and become like children, you will never enter the Kingdom of heaven.* [4] *The greatest in the Kingdom of heaven is the one who humbles himself and becomes like this child.* [5] *And whoever welcomes in my name one such child as this, welcomes me."*

One of the most difficult lessons in life is that God loves a faithful simplicity. Natural humanity wishes to find some measure by which it can assure itself of its superiority. The question put to Jesus by his disciples is just such a sign. The disciples had traveled with Jesus long enough to realize that he did not set up competitive patterns among people. Yet their desire to see where they stood brought them to ask nevertheless.

It must have been a shock to see Jesus take someone at the beginning of life as the model of greatness. In fact, even more than they bargained for, they were told that it is only as a child that one can enter the Kingdom.

Much has been written and said on what it means to become as a child. Children have certain qualities that are not worth imitating, so it is left to the imagination of the hearer exactly what it is about children that Jesus was commending.

Perhaps the quality that is held up is the ability of a child to trust those responsible for his or her care. A young man tells the story of how his uncles used to drop him from the second floor window to catch him on the porch below. If they should have missed, there was another twenty foot drop to the ground. And yet he remembers his complete trust that he would be caught. Today as an adult he would not have that same confidence in his uncles. It is probably this quality of children that people must have to be a part of the Kingdom of God.

Jesus placed himself in the shoes of children in verse 5. His face can be seen in the face of any child. And one can help him by helping any child.

18:6-9

[6] *"If anyone should cause one of these little ones to turn away from his faith in me, it would be better for that man to have a large millstone tied around his neck and be drowned in the deep sea. [7] How terrible for the world that there are things that make people turn away! Such things will always happen — but how terrible for the one who causes them!*

[8] *"If your hand or your foot makes you turn away, cut it off and throw it away! It is better for you to enter life without a hand or a foot than to keep both hands and both feet and be thrown into the eternal fire. [9] And if your eye makes you turn away, take it out and throw it away! It is better for you to enter life with only one eye than to keep both eyes and be thrown into the fire of hell."*

Life is a great opportunity. There are experiences to be enjoy in this world — at every age — that the angels would love to have. To be born into this world, given a fighting chance as a child, is a fantastic blessing.

But life is not a free ride. God the creator requires an accounting of the use made of life. One of the most grievous sins, as described by Jesus, is the tempting of children. They would be better off executed than to become an agent of sin.

Jesus also focused the matter more precisely for each individual. Amputation and mutilation is superior to the punishment that awaits such a one. (Punishment in the eternal fire does not necessarily mean the punishment is eternal, but that the fire is eternal.)

Some misguided souls have actually cut off a hand or put out an eye under the influence of this saying. They should have realized that Jesus knew the cause of sin was in the heart. Here he is indicating the seriousness of the circumstances, not urging literal mutilation.

18:10-14

[10] *"See that you don't despise any of these little ones. Their angels in heaven, I tell you, are always in the presence of my Father in heaven. [11] (For the Son of Man came to save the lost.)*

[12] *"What do you think? What will a man do who has one hundred sheep and one of them gets lost? He will leave the other ninety-nine*

grazing on the hillside and go to look for the lost sheep. [13] When he finds it, I tell you, he feels far happier over this one sheep than over the ninety-nine that did not get lost. [14] In just the same way your Father in heaven does not want any of these little ones to be lost."

An underlining of the importance of the little ones is provided by the fact that their guardian angels are about the highest ranking angels there are, indicated by the fact that they are privileged to see the face of God. The idea behind this text is often depicted in Christian art, but it is seldom discussed. Each person has a guardian angel, some people perhaps need more than one. The most overworked angels are those responsible for little children, because of all of the scrapes little ones get in on.

The people who listened to Jesus knew about the angels. But what was surprising in what he said was his estimation of these spiritual babysitters. In modern society one would not normally rank a babysitter with a secretary of state, for example. But Jesus ranked heavenly babysitters above cabinet members. It was another indication of God's very high evaluation of children.

In the parable of the lost sheep, Jesus apparently intended to convey God's special concern for the lost. In Matthew this parable is applied to the little ones, unlike Luke and the Gospel of Thomas. Natural humanity tends to quarrel with this parable, because the values of natural humanity differ from God's values. He does not think it is wise to leave the ninety-nine unattended. A wolf or lion could come and destroy quite a few of them and scatter the rest.

In the version of the parable told in the Gospel of Thomas, the story is changed slightly to make the one that wandered off the largest and fattest. In this way it is made to seem reasonable that the shepherd would seek him. And the shepherd says: "I love you more than the ninety-nine." But God does not think in such a way. He went after the lost. He has greater joy over finding the one than over the ninety-nine. But it does not say he loved it more. He does not say it was fatter. Only that it was lost. And the shepherd sought it.

It is a real source of comfort to everyone that God is like that.

18:15-17

[15] "If your brother sins against you, go to him and show him his fault. But do it privately, just between yourselves. If he listens to you, you have won your brother back. [16] But if he will not listen to you, take one or two other persons with you, so that 'every accusation may be upheld by the testimony of two or three witnesses,' as the scripture says. [17] But if he will not listen to them, then tell the whole thing to the church. And then, if he will not listen to the church, treat him as though he were a foreigner or a tax collector."

This passage is used by many Christian churches as a disciplinary procedure in the case of difficulty with a member. In it Jesus showed a sensitivity toward the wrongdoer (first he is approached privately). Further, he recognized that people can honestly differ in how they hear, so he provided for witnesses to every accusation, following Mosaic Law (Deuteronomy 19:15). Next if there is no reconciliation, the matter is to be brought before the full community for a hearng. And if that has no results, the person is to be expelled from the community.

This is a very democratic procedure which vests the greatest power in the community at large. It inherited from Israel a sense of the importance of all citizens far in advance of Greece, Rome, and Egypt, for example.

18:18-20

[18] "And so I tell all of you: what you prohibit on earth will be prohibited in heaven; what you permit on earth will be permitted in heaven.

[19] "And I tell you more: whenever two of you on earth agree about anything you pray for, it will be done for you by my Father in heaven. [20] For where two or three come together in my name, I am there with them."

Earlier Peter was given the power to bind and to loose. Here that same power is extended to all the disciples. It is an awesome thing that fallible human beings are given the power to bind in heaven.

God is so willing to share his power with the community that he is willing to let Christians acting in concert shape his will. His presence is guaranteed whenever even two or three Christians gather. Never before or since had a God made himself so accessible.

18:21-27

[21] *Then Peter came to Jesus and asked, "Lord, how many times can my brother sin against me and I have to forgive him? Seven times?"* [22] *"No, not seven times," answered Jesus, "but seventy times seven.* [23] *Because the Kingdom of heaven is like a king who decided to check on his servants' accounts.* [24] *He had just begun to do so when one of them was brought in who owed him millions of dollars.* [25] *The servant did not have enough to pay his debt, so his master ordered him to be sold as a slave, with his wife and his children and all that he had, in order to pay the debt.* [26] *The servant fell on his knees before his master. 'Be patient with me,' he begged, 'and I will pay you everything.'* [27] *The master felt sorry for him, so he forgave him the debt and let him go.*

When Peter asked Jesus about forgiveness, he anticipated from what he had heard from Jesus already that Jesus would be generous about forgiveness. To suggest forgiving someone seven times when sinned against is really stretching it. Think about a person who promises to meet another for lunch, and then does not show up. And this repeated itself six times. It is the extremely rare person who would not have scratched the other from his or her list.

But Jesus said that we are never to give up. Seventy times seven means beyond counting. Then in his typical fashion he told a story to illustrate it.

18:28-35

[28] *"The man went out and met one of his fellow servants who owed him a few dollars. He grabbed him and started choking him. 'Pay back what you owe me!' he said.* [29] *His fellow servant fell down and begged him, 'Be patient with me and I will pay you back!'* [30] *But he would not; instead, he had him thrown into jail until he should pay the debt.* [31] *When the other servants saw what had happened, they were very upset, and went to their master and told him everything.* [32] *So the master called the servant in. 'You worthless slave!' he said. 'I forgave you the whole amount you owed me, just because you asked me to.* [33] *You should have had mercy on your fellow servant, just as I had mercy on*

you.' [34] The master was very angry, and he sent the servant to jail to be punished until he should pay back the whole amount."

[35] And Jesus concluded, "That is how my Father in heaven will treat you if you do not forgive your brother, every one of you, from your heart."

This is one of the most straightforward stories Jesus has told. The point is that he who forgives will be forgiven by God. And he who does not forgive will not be forgiven. Since all are sinners before God, the way of perfect holiness is not a route to God. The only route to a relationship is the route of forgiveness and acceptance, which must flow in all directions.

Verse 34 in the parable has been used as one of the proof texts for purgatory. It is dangerous, however, to take a detail from a parable and assume it can be translated directly into the real world.

Matthew 19

Matthew 19:1-6

[1] When Jesus finished saying these things, he left Galilee and went to the territory of Judea, on the other side of the Jordan River. [2] Large crowds followed him, and he healed them there.

[3] Some Pharisees came to him and tried to trap him by asking, "Does our Law allow a man to divorce his wife for any reason he wished?"

[4] Jesus answered, "Haven't you read this scripture? 'In the beginning the Creator made them male and female, [5] and said, "For this reason a man will leave his father and mother and unite with his wife, and the two will become one." ' [6] So they are no longer two, but one. Man must not separate, then, what God has joined together."

Without much fanfare, Jesus entered Judaean territory. By his summary phrase "when Jesus finished saying these things," Matthew indicates that he knows this represents a significant shift. Galilee was a territory of mixed religion. It had Jews, but it also had Gentiles. Religious tolerance was greater and the influence of official religious leadership less. It had been Jewish for less than 200 years.

In Judea it was a different story. It was the territory of Jerusalem. Its heritage in Judaism was a continuous one back to the occupation of the land under Joshua. It had few Gentiles. Official religious interests were strongly represented.

The rigor of the Judaean climate is illustrated by what happened next. While he continued to attract as large a following among Judaeans as he had among Galileans, Jesus found immediate opposition from Pharisees. They raised a question about divorce, an issue on which the Pharisees and the Sadducees differed. The Pharisees allowed for divorce even for poor cooking, whereas the Sadducees insisted the grounds must be weighty.

Whatever Jesus' answer, he would displease someone. It is just the kind of question every politician seeks to avoid.

But Jesus took a very strong position, the strongest

to have emerged within Judaism to that point. He argued from Genesis 2:24 that the union of man and woman in marriage by God cannot be separated by man. Marriage is an irreversible process.

19:7-12

[7] *The Pharisees asked him, "Why, then, did Moses give the commandment for a man to give his wife a divorce notice and send her away?"*

[8] *Jesus answered, "Moses gave you permission to divorce your wives because you are so hard to teach. But it was not this way at the time of creation.* [9] *I tell you, then that any man who divorces his wife, and she has not been unfaithful, commits adultery if he marries some other woman."*

[10] *His disciples said to him, "If this is the way it is between a man and his wife, it is better not to marry."*

[11] *Jesus answered, "This teaching does not apply to everyone, but only to those to whom God has given it.* [12] *For there are different reasons why men cannot marry: some, because they were born that way; others, because men made them that way; and others do not marry because of the Kingdom of heaven. Let him who can do it accept this teaching."*

The radical position Jesus took regarding marriage is revealed by the Pharisee's citation of Deuteronomy 24, where the Law of Moses provided for divorce. Jesus responded by describing the Law at this point as a kind of interim ethic due to the hard-headedness of humanity rather than any expression of the will of God. Jesus allowed for divorce only for adultery according to Matthew. According to Mark 10:11, there are no legitimate grounds for divorce.

The response of the disciples indicates how shocked they were at what Jesus said. If marriage is that binding, then people would be better off not marrying in the first place.

Verse 11 probably means that Jesus recognized that the view of marriage he held up was ideal, and not possible for everyone because of human sin. But he does not wish to credit God with divorce, as if that is God's will. God's will for humanity is the oneness and fullness that the two sexes can achieve in union with one another.

Anything less than marriage violates God's intention in creation.

A second theme, that of celibacy, is introduced by the disciples' hesitation concerning such high stakes in marriage. It is one of the more difficult and more misunderstood passages in the Bible. The English translation above does not even use the central word of the passage, "eunuch."

There are three types of eunuchs, said Jesus. (A eunuch is an impotent male.)

1. There are men born impotent.
2. There are men who have been made eunuchs by others.
3. There are those who make themselves eunuchs for the sake of the Kingdom.

The early Christian theologian Origen took this saying literally and castrated himself. For his act he was excommunicated, indicating that most of his church did not read this saying so literally. If the term is to be understood figuratively in the third part, then such an interpretation must be considered for two and one. Two, however, must be literal. One could figuratively refer to men who have no romantic interest in women. Three could mean those people who have foresworn marriage because of their commitment to the Kingdom.

19:13-15

[13] Some people brought children to Jesus for him to place his hands on them and pray, but the disciples scolded those people. [14] Jesus said, "Let the chldren come to me, and do not stop them, because the Kingdom of heaven belongs to such as these."
[15] He placed his hands on them and left.

The importance of children was not an incidental theme to Jesus' message. In this story the disciples' assumption that the children should take second place to more pressing concerns was not shared by Jesus. But it is typical of the adult world. It is typical but not exclusive, because there were the friends of the children who brought them for a blessing. Most all children have been lucky enough to meet one such person in their life, an uncle or neighbor who really hears them when they talk and actually believes they are the most important people on earth.

The mystery of the Kingdom is revealed in children. It is made up of such a kind of people as they. To underline his meaning, Jesus blessed them and left.

19:16-26

[16] *Once a man came to Jesus. "Teacher," he asked, "what good thing must I do to receive eternal life?"*

[17] *"Why do you ask me concerning what is good?" answered Jesus. "There is only One who is good. Keep the commandments if you want to enter life."*

[18] *"What commandments?" he asked*

Jesus answered, "Do not murder; do not commit adultery; do not steal; do not lie; [19] honor your father and mother; and love your fellow-man as yourself."

[20] *"I have obeyed all these commandments," the young man replied. "What else do I need?"*

[21] *Jesus said to him, "If you want to be perfect, go and sell all you have and give the money to the poor, and you will have riches in heaven; then come and follow me."*

[22] *When the young man heard this he went away sad, because he was very rich.*

[23] *Jesus then said to his disciples. "It will be very hard, I tell you, for a rich man to enter the Kingdom of heaven. [24] I tell you something else: it is much harder for a rich man to enter the Kingdom of God than for a camel to go through the eye of a needle."*

[25] *When the disciples heard this they were completely amazed. "Who can be saved, then?" they asked.*

[26] *Jesus looked straight at them and answered, "This is impossible for men; but for God everything is possible."*

This is a rich story. It contains Jesus' refusal to accept the attribute good because he though it ought to be used only for God, thereby revealing that he did not consider himself and God one and the same, at least during his earthly sojourn. This, however, is a side issue to the story.

A religious man wanted to assure himself of eternal life. Jesus did not ask anything different from the moral law. The man assured Jesus he had kept these, but felt that he still lacked something.

"If you want to be perfect (complete)," Jesus said.

The meaning of this phrase has been interpreted differently at different times. The second century Christian catechism recognized two standards for Christians, one for perfection, one for ordinary Christians. The church as it developed monastaries tended to continue the idea of two types of Christians.

After the Reformation, it was hard for people to even see that the talk is about perfection. How can sinful man be perfect, it is asked?

Jesus did not often answer hard theological questions. He saw what stood between this man and what he was seeking (perfection, completeness). He offered him a rich gift, indeed, to be one of his disciples. But the man could not part with his possessions.

The comment Jesus made when the rich man left was properly understood by the disciples. A camel obviously cannot get more than a whisker through the eye of a needle. Did that mean that no one can be saved? The disciples did not ask only about the rich, but about all. And about all, Jesus said, salvation is impossible. That is, it is impossible for humanity to achieve by its own efforts. This text perhaps anticipates why it was necessary for Jesus to die, that is, as God's way of making the impossible possible.

19:27-30

[27] *Then Peter spoke up. "Look," he said, "we have left everything and followed you. What will we have?"*

[28] *Jesus said to them, "I tell you this: when the Son of Man sits on his glorious throne in the New Age, then you twelve followers of mine will also sit on thrones, to judge the twelve tribes of Israel.* [29] *And every one who has left houses or brothers or sisters or father or mother or children or fields for my sake, will receive a hundred times more, and will be given eternal life.* [30] *But many who now are first will be last, and many who now are last will be first."*

The promise of a rich reward for sacrifices made in God's name is central to the New Testament. Many theologians wince at this, because they do not like the possibility that people will do good only to obtain a reward. That problem did not seem to bother Jesus.

The disciples would have cabinet rank in the New Age. Everyone who has made sacrifices will be richly rewarded.

Verse 30 is a reminder that life is long, and commitment can waver. Followers of Jesus today are not necessarily so in a decade. And blessed are those who persevere until the end.

124

Matthew 20

Matthew 20:1-16

[1] *"The Kingdom of heaven is like the owner of a vineyard who went out early in the morning to hire some men to work in his vineyard. [2] He agreed to pay them the regular wage, a silver coin a day, and sent them to work in his vineyard. [3] He went out again to the market place at nine o'clock and saw some men standing there doing nothing, [4] so he told them, 'You also go to work in the vineyard, and I will pay you a fair wage.' [5] So they went. Then at twelve o'clock and again at three o'clock he did the same thing. [6] It was nearly five o'clock when he went to the market place and saw some other men still standing there. 'Why are you wasting the whole day here doing nothing?' he asked them. [7] 'It is because no one hired us,' they answered. 'Well, then, you also go to work in the vineyard,' he told them.*

[8] *"When evening came, the owner told his foreman, 'Call the workers and pay them their wages, starting with those who were hired last, and ending with those who were hired first.' [9] The men who had begun to work at five o'clock were paid a silver coin each. [10] So when the men who were the first to be hired came to be paid, they thought they would get more; but they too were given a silver coin each. [11] They took their money and started grumbling against the employer. [12] 'These men who were hired last worked only one hour,' they said, 'while we put up with a whole day's work in the hot sun — yet you paid them the same as you paid us!' [13] 'Listen, friend,' the owner answered one of them. 'I have not cheated you. After all, you agreed to do a day's work for a silver coin. [14] Now, take your pay and go home. I want to give this man who was hired last as much as I have given you. [15] Don't I have the right to do as I wish with my own money? Or are you jealous because I am generous?' "*

[16] *And Jesus concluded, "So those who are last will be first, and those who are first will be last."*

This parable of the Kingdom generally makes people angry. Most see themselves in the situation of the people who have labored the entire day, only to discover that there were those who worked less, including some who worked only an hour. They quite readily see themselves tired from a long day for a fair wage, resenting that someone else got the same without even working up a sweat.

Jesus was not talking about labor practices. He was not making recommendations for employers. But he was seeking to tell something about God's Kingdom.

The workers reacted in jealousy because someone

else had good fortune. In fact, those who worked the entire day received a fair wage and the wage they were promised. They were in no way diminished by the good fortune of others.

The parable teaches that God's ways are not man's ways. He stands ready to extend opportunity after opportunity to all humankind. Even those who came to the hiring market late were blessed through the vineyard owner's generosity with a day's wage for their family and their other needs.

In like manner God does not tire of the human race. His covenants with Israel and with the church have given neither an exclusive claim upon him. God can — and does — reach out to all sorts and conditions of humanity. He will be fair. But he will not allow fairness to prevent him from all of his purposes in the unfolding of his will.

20:17-19

[17] *As Jesus was going up to Jerusalem he took the twelve disciples aside and spoke to them privately, as they walked along.* [18] *"Listen," he told them, "we are going up to Jerusalem, where the Son of Man will be handed over to the chief priests and the teachers of the Law. They will condemn him to death* [19] *and then hand him over to the Gentiles, who will make fun of him, whip him, and nail him to the cross; and on the third day he will be raised to life."*

Jesus did not allow his disciples to forget that his mission would result in his going through death in Jerusalem. This time the prediction is a bit more detailed, including the participation of both Jewish and Gentile leaders in his condemnation, as well as the fact that it would be a torturous death.

20:20-28

[20] *Then the mother of Zebedee's sons came to Jesus with her sons, bowed before him, and asked him for a favor.*

[21] *"What do you want?" Jesus asked her.*

She answered, "Promise that these two sons of mine will sit at your right and your left when you are King."

[22] *"You don't know what you are asking for," Jesus answered them. "Can you drink the cup that I am about to drink?"*

"We can," they answered.

126

[23] "You will indeed drink from my cup," Jesus told them, "but I do not have the right to choose who will sit at my right and my left. These places belong to those for whom my Father has prepared them."

[24] When the other ten disciples heard about this they became angry with the two brothers. [25] So Jesus called them all together to him and said, "You know that the rulers have power over the people, and their leaders rule over them. [26] This, however, is not the way it shall be among you. If one of you wants to be great, he must be the servant of the rest; [27] and if one of you wants to be first, he must be your slave — [28] like the Son of Man, who did not come to be served, but to serve and to give his life to redeem many people."

The path to glory in Christianity leads through a cross. The mother of two of Jesus' disciples, perhaps impressed by his success, expected him to be an earthly King. She wanted to be sure that they would play a major role in his Kingdom; this would no doubt make her own future secure and her heart overflow with pride.

Jesus tested her by asking them whether they were able to drink the cup that he was to drink (no doubt referring to his coming suffering and death). They may or may not have understood the question. If they did, they answered much too quickly in view of the trials that lay ahead.

He assured them that he was not in a position to assign those positions, that such was God's prerogative.

He did, however, take one more opportunity to instruct the disciples in God's way. Power and position with God is not attained or exercised as among the great of this world. Service and humility are the highest goods. Preferment does not come to the proud. The model for the Christian is the life-course of Jesus, who although he was in the heights of heaven, did not come into the world for adoration but to give, even to the point of giving his own life.

20:29-34

[29] As they were leaving Jericho a large crowd followed Jesus. [30] Two blind men who were sitting by the road heard that Jesus was passing by, so they began to shout, "Son of David! Have mercy on us, sir!"

[31] The crowd scolded them and told them to be quiet. But they shouted even more loudly, "Son of David! Have mercy on us, sir!"

[32] Jesus stopped and called them. "What do you want me to do for you?" he asked them.

[33] "Sir," they answered, "we want you to open our eyes!"

[34] Jesus had pity on them and touched their eyes; at once they were able to see, and followed him.

The tempo of the story is quickening. The crowds grow. They sense a specialness about Jesus, and they tend to interpret it as the beginning of a new earthly kingdom, excelling the political and cultural heights of the Davidic Kingdom of old.

The crowd no longer has time for the lives of a couple of blind derelicts by the roadside. More important things are in the wind. It's the crowd therefore that sought to silence two blind beggars who have more immediate need of Jesus' help. That saw him as David's son, but needed something today.

And Jesus, moved by pity for their plight, did not disappoint them.

Matthew 21

Matthew 21:1-7

[1] *As they approached Jerusalem, they came to Bethphage, at the Mount of Olives. There Jesus sent two of the disciples on ahead* [2] *with these instructions, "Go to the village there ahead of you, and at once you will find a donkey tied up and her colt with her. Untie them and bring them to me.* [3] *And if anyone says anything, tell him, 'The Master needs them'; and he will let them go at once."*
[4] *This happened to make come true what the prophet had said:*
[5] *"Tell the city of Zion,*
Now your king is coming to you.
He is gentle and rides on a donkey,
on a colt, the foal of a donkey."
[6] *So the disciples went ahead and did what Jesus had told them to do:* [7] *they brought the donkey and the colt, threw their cloaks over them, and Jesus got on.*

Jesus knew that his entry into Jerusalem was a very special occasion. He could have chosen to come into the city like any ordinary citizen. But he, in the fashion of a presidential candidate in a motorcade, made provision for a grand entrance into the city.

The incident with the colt is another reminder that in the case of Jesus one deals with a mysterious figure. Some commentators have gone to great lengths to argue that Jesus had set this up in advance. Or that he had a friend who he knew kept his donkey there at the edge of town. Such speculations are unlikely, but not impossible.

An odd feature of the story is what many see as Matthew's misunderstanding of the Zecharah 9:9 passage. When it says your King comes "on a donkey, on a colt, the foal of a donkey," it is probably not suggesting that Jesus is sitting on two animals, but the animal is simply mentioned twice. This is typical of Hebrew poetical style. Both Luke and Mark report it as one animal. Likely Matthew's concern for an exact fulfillment of Scripture, which this passage in fact is, has led him to create this rather odd picture of Jesus sitting on two animals.

21:8-11

[8] *A great crowd of people spread their cloaks on the road, while others cut branches from the trees and spread them on the road. [9] The crowds walking in front of Jesus and the crowds walking behind began to shout, "Praise to David's Son! God bless him who comes in the name of the Lord! Praise be to God!"*

[10] *When Jesus entered Jerusalem the whole city was thrown in an uproar. "Who is he?" the people asked.*

[11] *"This is the prophet Jesus, from Nazareth of Galilee," the crowds answered.*

The gesture of Jesus was not lost on the crowds thronging to Jerusalem to celebrate the Passover, the anniversary of the time when God caused the angel of death to pass over the children of Israel but to smite the Eyptians. They hailed him again as David's Son. Many had seen his wonderful deeds. Many had heard of him. But most of his activity had been carried out in the area of Galilee. Now his presence at a time of festival — when the city was filled with pilgrims from throughout the known world — threw the city into an intense excitement.

Verse 11 calls Jesus of Nazareth. That denotes the town of his upbringing, just as many family names in this day have come from place names. The fact that he is called a prophet indicates that the crowd still had not decided he was the Messiah, but they were indeed granting him a lofty title.

21:12-17

[12] *Jesus went into the temple and drove out all those who bought and sold in the temple; he overturned the tables of the moneychangers and the stools of those who sold pigeons, [13] and said to them, "It is written in the Scriptures that God said, 'My house will be called a house of prayer.' But you are making it a hideout for thieves!"*

[14] *The blind and the crippled came to him in the temple and he healed them. [15] The chief priests and the teachers of the Law became angry when they saw the wonderful things he was doing, and the children shouting and crying in the temple, "Praise to David's Son!"*

[16] *So they said to Jesus, "Do you hear what they are saying?"*

"Indeed I do," answered Jesus. "Haven't you ever read this scripture? 'You have trained children and babies to offer perfect praise.' "

[17] *Jesus left them and went out of the city to Bethany, where he spent the night.*

130 .

Jesus' initial act in the city of Jerusalem was to drive out those who changed money for offering and those who sold pigeons for sacrifice. Unless one has traveled outside of this country, he or she has not had that experience of having to buy a new currency every time one enters a new country. For every exchange, a certain percentage is charged as commission for the dealer. Certain money changers charge a fair amount more than others.

When Jewish pilgrims who lived outside Palestine came for the festival and wished to have money to spend, they needed to get it at the temple. Ancient temples were also the treasuries for their respective nations. Jesus apparently felt that the temple was more of a house of business than a house of prayer. The birds were used for sacrifice. While it was perfectly legitimate to bring one from home, travelers from a great distance found it more convenient to buy one at Jerusalem. These dealers were driven out with the rest.

Jesus has often been pictured as a pacifist. He did not raise a finger to defend himself. But in this case he was a man of violence. It should be noted, however, that it was violence against goods and not people. He overturned tables and stools, but he did not physically abuse another person. His zeal, even for God, did not lead him to lay a finger on another human being in anger.

When he had cleared the temple, he used it for its intended purpose, as a place of healing. His critics expected him to repudiate those who called him David's Son (Messiah). Instead he saw it as a fulfillment of the Scriptures (Psalms 8:1-2).

Jesus probably was spending the night outside of the city because of the crush of pilgrims for Passover.

21:18-22

[18] *On his way back to the city, early next morning, Jesus was hungry. [19] He saw a fig tree by the side of the road and went to it, but found nothing on it except leaves. So he said to the tree, "You will never again bear fruit!" At once the fig tree dried up.*

[20] *The disciples saw this and were astounded. "How did the fig tree*

131

dry up so quickly?" they asked.

[21] "Remember this!" Jesus answered. "If you believe, and do not doubt, you will be able to do what I have done to this fig tree; not only this, you will even be able to say to this hill, 'Get up and throw yourself in the sea,' and it will. [22] If you believe, you will receive whatever you ask for in prayer."

The fate of the fig tree shows the awesome power of Jesus. He was up early and had not yet had breakfast. He saw the tree and hoped it would provide him a breakfast. It did not and he cursed it. And it dried up and died.

The story is significant in that it shows that Jesus could have used his awesome power in a variety of ways. Some gifted people have used their gifts primarily for their own advantage. Jesus did not, but in a small way (big to the fig tree) one sees here how he might have.

Jesus used the occasion to teach. Such awesome power is available to everyone through the power of prayer. In the words of a recent evangelism campaign, "God still makes house calls."

21:23-27

[23] Jesus came back to the temple; and as he taught, the chief priests and the Jewish elders came to him and asked, "What right do you have to do these things? Who gave you this right?"

[24] Jesus answered them, "I will ask you just one question, and if you give me an answer I will tell you what right I have to do these things. [25] Where did John's right to baptize come from: from God or from men?"

They started to argue among themselves, "What shall we say? If we answer, 'from God,' he will say to us, 'Why, then, did you not believe John?' [26] But if we say, 'From men,' we are afraid of what the people might do, because they are all convinced that John was a prophet." [27] So they answered Jesus, "We don't know."

And he said to them, "Neither will I tell you, then, by what right I do these things."

Jesus returned to the temple which he had the day before cleansed. The fact that he was not immediately placed under arrest indicates the restraint of the Jewish leadership and the seriousness with which the people took men and women of religious intensity. But Jesus was approached by the leadership on the question of the authority upon which he acted.

The answer of Jesus, rather typical of him, was a counter-question: "What was the authority by which John baptized?" The question provided a problem to the leaders. Some in Judaism in Jesus' day were convinced that God no longer spoke directly to the people. He had revealed his Law to Moses. The age of prophecy was complete. Not all Jews, of course, took such a position. But the two major parties tended toward this position. The position they took is typical of most Christian churches today if someone says that God has spoken to him. The Spirit spoke once, but no longer, is their attitude.

The leaders suspected that John had not experienced divine revelation. But they hesitated to say so because the people believed John had spoken the Word of God. It is also typical today that the ordinary people are more ready to give a new voice a hearing than those that hold their power by interpreting the past.

Since the leaders would not commit themselves, neither would Jesus. The situation was full of tension. The leaders did not move against Jesus. But he also did not back down an inch. In fact, he embarrassed them by bringing up the popular John in the presence of the people.

21:28-32

[28] "Now, what do you think? There was a man who had two sons. He went to the older one and said, 'Son, go work in the vineyard today.' [29] 'I don't want to,' he answered, but later he changed his mind and went to the vineyard. [30] Then the father went to the other son and said the same thing. 'Yes, sir,' he answered, but he did not go. [31] Which one of the two did what his father wanted?"

"The older one," they answered.

"And I tell you this," Jesus said to them. "The tax collectors and the prostitutes are going into the Kingdom of God ahead of you. [32] For John the Baptist came to you showing you the right path to take, and you would not believe him; but the tax collectors and the prostitutes believed him. Even when you saw this you did not change your minds later on and believe him."

The parable of the two sons again shows Jesus' preference for action over words. Neither son would prevent his father from having premature grey hair. But the hearers would no doubt agree that the person who came through in the end is the better of the two.

Jesus applied the parable specifically to those who considered themselves righteous in the religious community. They had been unmoved by John's preaching, perhaps thinking that it applied to someone else but not to them. Therefore, Jesus saw, and had discovered in his own work, that those who had considered themselves righteous failed to pick up on the golden opportunity before them. But obvious sinners were taking the opportunity to mend their ways.

21:33-41

[33] "Listen to another parable," Jesus said. "There was a landowner who planted a vineyard, put a fence around it, dug a hole for the winepress, and built a watchtower. Then he rented the vineyard to tenants and left home on a trip. [34] When the time came to harvest the grapes he sent his slaves to the tenants to receive his share. [35] The tenants grabbed his slaves, beat one, killed another, and stoned another. [36] Again the man sent other slaves, more than the first time, and the tenants treated them the same way. [37] Last of all he sent them his son. 'Surely they will respect my son,' he said. [38] But when the tenants saw the son they said to themselves, 'This is the owner's son. Come on, let us kill him, and we will get his property!' [39] So they grabbed him, threw him out of the vineyard, and killed him.

[40] "Now, when the owner of the vineyard comes, what will he do to those tenants?" Jesus asked.

[41] "He will certainly kill those evil men," they answered, "and rent the vineyard out to other tenants, who will give him his share of the harvest at the right time."

The parables directed at the religious and political leadership become more pointed as this section of the Gospel proceeds. This parable is a clear allegory of the experience of God with Israel. It is very pointed and the hearers would no doubt have heard the following message.

God has given responsibility for Israel into certain hands. When he has sent his own among them(prophets) they have been mistreated and killed. Even when he sent his son, they sought to control their own destiny by killing the son.

He led his hearers to pronounce sentence upon themselves and Jerusalem, quite unaware of what they were doing. In verse 41 they even anticipate the mission to the Gentiles.

21:42-46

[42] *Jesus said to them, "Haven't you ever read what the Scriptures say?*
The very stone which the builders rejected
turned out to be the most important stone.
This was done by the Lord;
how wonderful it is!
[43] *"And so I tell you," added Jesus, "the Kingdom of God will be taken away from you and be given to a people who will produce the proper fruits. (44) Whoever falls on this stone will be broken to pieces; and if the stone falls on someone it will crush him to dust."*
[45] *The chief priests and the Pharisees heard Jesus' parables and knew that he was talking about them, [46] so they tried to arrest him. but they were afraid of the crowds, who considered Jesus to be a prophet.*

And Jesus drove the argument home by citing Psalms 118:22-23. The rejection was not unexpected, and a great reversal is in store. A stone not even though good enough for the structure will come to play a central role.

And finally Jesus stated his meaning without parables. The Kingdom will be taken from those to whom he was speaking and given to those who will produce fruits. (Whether the tax collectors and harlots or Gentiles are meant here is not clear.)

Verse 44 probably is added from the parallel account in Luke. It is a further development of the thought about Jesus as the cornerstone.

The chief priests and Pharisees were affronted by Jesus' attack. They made a move to arrest him but did not go through with it because of the high standing Jesus still enjoyed with the crowds.

Matthew 22

Matthew 22:1-14

[1] Jesus again used parables in talking to the people. [2] "The Kingdom of heaven is like a king who prepared a wedding feast for his son. [3] He sent his servants to tell the invited guests to come to the feast, but they did not want to come. [4] So he sent other servants with the message: 'Tell the guests, "My feast is ready now; my steers and prize calves have been butchered, and everything is ready. Come to the wedding feast!"' [5] But the invited guests paid no attention and went about their business: one went to his farm, the other to his store, [6] while others grabbed the servants, beat them, and killed them. [7] The king was very angry; he sent his soldiers, who killed those murderers and burned down their city. [8] Then he called his servants. 'My wedding feast is ready,' he said, 'but the people I invited did not deserve it. [9] Now go to the main streets and invite to the feast as many people as you find.' [10] So the servants went out into the streets and gathered all the people they could find, good and bad alike; and the wedding hall was filled with people.

[11] "The king went in to look at the guests and he saw a man who was not wearing wedding clothes. [12] 'Friend, how did you get in here without wedding clothes?' the king asked him. But the man said nothing. [13] Then the king told the servants, 'Tie him up hand and foot and throw him outside in the dark. There he will cry and gnash his teeth.'"

[14] And Jesus concluded, "For many are invited, but few are chosen."

One of the best evidenced parables available for study is that of the marriage feast. It has been handed down separately and had a different development in Matthew, Luke, and the Gospel of Thomas. Matthew has attached, or found attached, an additional parable in verses 11-13.

The basic meaning of the parable as originally told treats of people who refuse an invitation for a variety of reasons. When the man hears of it he makes sure that other guests are invited, so that he may have his banquet.

The parable has certain emphases in each version. In Luke the servant is sent out twice to get enough guests (according to commentators, first the have nots in Israel, then the Gentiles). In the Gospel of Thomas, each person that has an excuse is a business person. And at the end of the parable business people are condemned.

Here in Matthew the parable sounds a bit like the parable of the wicked tenants. The host is a King. The banquet is mammoth. There is murder in the air. Guests kill servants and the King kills the murderers and burns their city. Then others, both good and bad, are brought in to enjoy the banquet. It may be that the placement of the parable here in the Jerusalem period moved it in the direction of an allegory of the death of the prophets and the destruction of Jerusalem.

The story of the wedding garment probably means that no one can participate in the Kingdom without a garment of righteousness. The interloper ends up in the outer darkness.

Verse 14 as a summary was used a number of places. It is not clear how it applies to this parable, since more were invited than came, and only one person was excluded.

22:15-22

[15] *The Pharisees went off and made a plan to trap Jesus with questions. [16] Then they sent some of their disciples and some members of Herod's party to Jesus. "Teacher," they said, "we know that you tell the truth. You teach the truth about God's will for man, without worrying about what people think, because you pay no attention to a man's status. [17] Tell us, then, what do you think? Is it against our Law to pay taxes to the Roman Emperor, or not?"*

[18] *Jesus was aware of their evil plan, however, and so he said, "You hypocrites! Why are you trying to trap me? [19] Show me the coin to pay the tax!"*

They brought him the coin, [20] and he asked them, "Whose face and name are these?"

[21] *"The Emperor's," they answered.*

So Jesus said to them, "Well, then, pay to the Emperor what belongs to him, and pay to God what belongs to God."

[22] *When they heard this, they were filled with wonder; and they left him and went away.*

An alliance between the Pharisees and the Herodians is odd. The Pharisees were devoutly religious and the Herodians devoutly political. The Pharisees saw Jesus as a religious menace and the Herodians feared his political popularity with the crowds. They had little time for one another. But their concern about Jesus was greater than their hatred for one another.

The question about taxes was a real trap. Most Jews resented the Roman bondage, represented by the hated tax that drained wealth from the country to enrich an already-sated Rome. Jesus understood the question as a trap. If he supported the tax, he would lose his popularity with the people. If he condemned it, he could be executed as a political revolutionary.

By the answer he gave he supported giving Caesar what he had already brought into the country, that is, currency. But by reminding people of their obligation to God, he said the political subordination does not prevent one from serving God. That is, the meaning of life is greater than political sovereignty.

And they could not dismiss Jesus as a Roman lackey or execute him as an insurrectionist.

22:23-33

[23] *That same day some Sadducees came to Jesus. [They are the ones who say that people will not rise from death.] [24] "Teacher," they said, "Moses taught: 'If a man who has no children dies, his brother must marry the widow so they can have children for the dead man.' [25] Now, there were seven brothers who used to live here. The oldest got married, and died without having children, so he left his widow to his brother. [26] The same thing happened to the second brother, to the third, and finally to all seven. [27] Last of all, the woman died. [28] Now, on the day when the dead rise to life, whose wife will she be? All of them had married her."*

[29] *Jesus answered them, "How wrong you are! It is because you don't know the Scriptures or God's power. [30] For when the dead rise to life they will be like the angels in heaven, and men and women will not marry. [31] Now, as for the dead rising to life: haven't you ever read what God has told you? He said, [32] 'I am the God of Abraham, the God of Isaac, and the God of Jacob.' This means that he is the God of the living, not of the dead."*

[33] *When the crowds heard this they were amazed at his teaching.*

The Sadducees were conservatives. They believed neither in resurrection nor angels. They attempted to show that belief in a life after death was ridiculous by reference to the woman who was married in turn to seven brothers. "Whose wife will she be in the resurrection?"

Christianity is grateful to the Sadducees for raising the question, for through it a fact of the resurrection life is revealed. In that life people will be like angels, they will not marry. Hence the question of the Sadducees was really not a problem.

Jesus anticipated the second question: What is the biblical basis for this teaching? For as it was said, the Sadducees were real conservatives. If it was not in the Bible, then it must not be true.

By way of answer, Jesus quoted Exodus 3:6. If God could say to Moses that he was the God of his ancestors the ancestors must be alive. The argument itself is less impressive than the fact that Jesus was so explicit about life after death, a central teaching of Christianity.

Jesus' statement that there is not marriage in the resurrection does not mean that loved ones cannot share together in the resurrection life. Souls that love, and that love one another, can never be truly separated.

22:34-40

[34] *When the Pharisees heard that Jesus had silenced the Sadducees, they came together, [35] and one of them, a teacher of the Law, tried to trap him with a question. [36] "Teacher," he asked, "which is the greatest commandment in the Law?"*

[37] Jesus answered, " 'You must love the Lord your God with all your heart, with all your soul, and with all your mind.' [38] This is the greatest and the most important commandment. [39] The second most important commandment is like it: 'You must love your fellow-man as yourself.' [40] The whole Law of Moses and the teahings of the prophets depend on these two commandments."

The questions continued. An inquiry from the Pharisees on the greatest commandment brought forth a thoughtful distillation of true religion. "Love God and love your neighbor as yourself."

The balance included here is wonderful, because it includes three loves. God is all in all. So he is the starting point and without the love of God there is always distortion. Love of neighbor is like a commandment. Humanity cannot do much for God. But so far, the help needed by people is practically infinite. And both study and experience have shown that love is the best help of all.

A recent study of a high crime area revealed one neighborhood where the percentage of people who had had a brush with the law was far below that area's average. An exhaustive series of interviews was done with the residents to find out what the difference was. In the interviews the name of a particular fifth grade teacher kept popping up. So the interview team started inquiring what it was particularly about this teacher. "She just loved us," was the reply the interviewer received. Love of neighbor is the twin of love of God.

And it is worth noting that Jesus said "Love your neighbor **as yourself.**" Every person loves himself or herself, from the smallest baby to the oldest citizen. Here the Law does not ask people to deny it. Just give the neighbor as good treatment as the self.

The Scriptures cited are Deuteronomy 6:5 (the Shema which is the great confession of every Jew) and Leviticus 19:18. The combination guards against loveless religion and godless humanitarianism.

22:41-46

[41] When the Pharisees gathered together, Jesus asked them, [42] "What do you think about the Messiah? Whose descendant is he?"

"He is David's descendant," they answered.

[43] "Why, then," Jesus asked, "did the Spirit inspire David to call him 'Lord'? Because David said,

[44] 'The Lord said to my Lord:

Sit here at my right side, until I put your enemies under your feet.'

[45] If, then, David called him 'Lord,' how can the Messiah be David's descendant?"

[46] No one was able to answer Jesus a single word, and from that day on no one dared ask him any more questions.

People in New Testament times believed that David was the author of all of the Psalms. Jesus' question to the Pharisees is built upon that foundation. If it is appropriate to simply interpret the Messiah as David's Son, argues Jesus, of whom is David speaking when he said, "The Lord (Yahweh) said to my Lord." Jesus' own conclusion is that he was speaking of the Messiah, in which case the standing of the Messiah in relation to David would be a great deal more than son or descendant.

This is another example of Jesus' attempt to raise the idea of the Messiah above that of the merely physical and political. It marks the end of a series of controversies with the various religious groups.

Matthew 23

Matthew 23:1-12

[1] Then Jesus spoke to the crowds and to his disciples. [2] "The teachers of the Law and the Pharisees," he said, "are the authorized interpreters of Moses' Law. [3] So you must obey and follow everything they tell you to do; do not, however, imitate their actions, because they do not practice what they preach. [4] They fix up heavy loads and tie them on men's backs, yet they aren't willing even to lift a finger to help them carry those loads. [5] They do everything just so people will see them. See how big are the containers with scripture verses on their foreheads and arms, and notice how long are the hems of their cloaks! [6] They love the best places at feasts and the reserved seats in the synagogues; [7] they love to be greeted with respect in the market places and have people call them 'Teacher.' [8] You must not be called 'Teacher,' because you are all brothers of one another and have only one Teacher. [9] And you must not call anyone here on earth 'Father,' because you have only the one Father in heaven. [10] Nor should you be called 'Leader,' because your one and only leader is the Messiah. [11] The greatest one among you must be your servant. [12] Whoever makes himself great will be humbled, and whoever humbles himself will be made great."

Almost this entire chapter is involved with Jesus' diatribe against the Pharisees. It is a good chapter that reveals Jesus' harsh judgments, yes, even hatred, against those who misuse the position of religious leadership. Two things ought to be remembered in reading it.

First, not all Pharisees were deserving of this condemnation. There were Pharisees in Jesus' time, and have been since, whose religion was profound and whose spirits were gentle. Second, most of the judgments Jesus hurled at the Pharisees could be leveled against the darker side of many clergy, elders, and Sunday School teachers today. By comparison to the Son of God, **all** are found wanting!

The initial critique against the Pharisees is not against their teaching, but their failure to live up to their own interpretation of the Law. They have a tendency to fall in love with their own position in the community. They like to be called rabbi.

Jesus opposed all titles because they infringed on

142

God's glory. God is teacher and father. The Messiah is
leader. Again and again he holds before his followers the
model of humility. Christians have been remiss in
remembering that.

23:13-22

[13] *"How terrible for you, teachers of the Law and Pharisees!
Hypocrites! You lock the door to the Kingdom of heaven in men's faces,
but you yourselves will not go in, and neither will you let people in who
are trying to go in!*

*[14] ("How terrible for you, teachers of the Law and Pharisees!
Hypocrites! You take advantage of widows and rob them of their homes,
and then make a show of saying long prayers! Because of this your
punishment will be all the worse!)*

*[15] "How terrible for you, teachers of the Law and Pharisees! You
sail the seas and cross whole countries to win one convert; and when you
succeed, you make him twice as deserving of going to hell as you
yourselves are!*

*[16] "How terrible for you, blind guides! You teach, 'If a man swears
by the temple he isn't bound by his vow; but if he swears by the gold in
the temple, he is bound.' [17] Blind fools! Which is more important, the
gold or the temple which makes the gold holy? [18] You also teach, 'If a
man swears by the altar, he isn't bound by his vow; but if he swears by
the gift on the altar, he is bound.' [19] How blind you are! Which is more
important, the gift or the altar which makes the gift holy? [20] So then,
when a man swears by the altar he is swearing by it and by all the gifts
on it; [21] and when a man swears by the temple he is swearing by it and
by God, the one who lives there; [22] and when a man swears by heaven
he is swearing by God's throne and by him who sits on it.*

Religious leaders who are lax or cynical do not make
gateways to the Kingdom, but barriers. There are few so
destructive as a bad priest or minister.

Clergy, too, have been known to make use of their
positions to get written into the wills of older people with
whom they spend time, working for their own advantage
while wearing a pious face. God is not mocked.

Modern sectarian movements are the most aggres-
sive in evangelism. It is sad to see the number of young
won to the lies of self-appointed prophets and interpreters of Scripture.

Jesus also hated casuistic distinctions. They make it
easier for the trained to cheat the simple. An oath is an
oath. And a person should be bound by it. There are not
greater and lesser degrees of integrity.

[23] *"How terrible for you, teachers of the Law and Pharisees! Hypocrites! You give to God one tenth even of the seasoning herbs, such as mint, dill, and cummin, but you neglect to obey the really important teachings of the Law, such as justice and mercy and honesty. These you should practice, without neglecting the others. [24] Blind guides! You strain a fly out of your drink, but swallow a camel!*

[25] *"How terrible for you, teachers of the Law and Pharisees! Hypocrites! You clean the outside of your cup and plate, while the inside is full of things you have gotten by violence and selfishness. [26] Blind Pharisee! Clean what is inside the cup first, and then the outside will be clean too!*

[27] *"How terrible for you, teachers of the Law and Pharisees! Hypocrites! You are like whitewashed tombs, which look fine on the outside, but are full of dead mens bones and rotten stuff on the inside. [28] In the same way, on the outside you appear to everybody as good, but inside you are full of hypocrisy and sins."*

Religion is always in danger of a preoccupation with minutia. Tithing, while it can provide the life blood for the mission of the church, is no substitute for a life lived in which the qualities of mercy, honesty, and justice are paramount. Distinctions in religion should be made, but there should be an eye to the importance of what is being discussed.

In matter of ritual purity, too, values have become reversed. Most important is the state of the soul, then of the communionware.

God knows the heart. There are people of all religious persuasions who walk about looking fine. Others can be impressed and say: "What a wonderful person is so and so." But if the quality is only skin deep, God knows. And it is God and not the neighbor who will be the final judge.

23:29-36

[29] *"How terrible for you, teachers of the Law and Pharisees! Hypocrites! You make fine tombs for the prophets, and decorate the monuments of those who lived good lives, [30] and you say, 'If we had lived long ago in the time of our ancestors, we would not have done what they did and killed the prophets.' [31] So you actually admit that you are the descendants of those who murdered the prophets! [32] Go on, then, and finish up what your ancestors started! [33] Snakes, and sons of snakes! How do you expect to escape from being condemned to hell? [34] And so I tell you: I will send you prophets and wise men and teachers; you will kill some of them, nail others to the cross, and whip others in your*

synagogues and chase them from town to town. [35] As a result, the punishment for the murder of all innocent men will fall on you, from the murder of innocent Abel to the murder of Zechariah, Barachiah's son, whom you murdered between the temple and the altar. [36] I tell you indeed: the punishment for all these will fall on the people of this day!"

This last section of the woes against the Pharisees is delivered in an almost prophetic frenzy. It sounds like Jeremiah in one of his sterner passages. It certainly places Jesus four square in the tradition of the Old Testament prophets.

The point in verse 29 about decorating the tombs of the prophets is indeed a good one. Many people find a prophet or social critic easier to appreciate after his death, when the intensity of his judgment can no longer be aimed at them.

Verse 34 seems typically prophetic, in that Jesus seems to be speaking the words of God. The prophecy predicts what is a part of the early experience of the Christian movement.

Verse 35 and 36 must be carefully handled. It is one thing for God to be involved in a controversy with his people. But it is quite another, and quite heinous, when Christians have understood a passage like this as encouragement to persecute Jews. For if Jews suffer in relation to failures in high purposes, the same holds true for Christians who have the same obligations in relation to God.

23:37-39

[37] "Jerusalem, Jerusalem! You kill the prophets and stone the messengers God has sent you! How many times have I wanted to put my arms around all your people, just as a hen gathers her chicks under her wings, but you would not let me! [38] Now your home will be completely forsaken. [39] From now on you will never see me again, I tell you, until you say, 'God bless him who comes in the name of the Lord.'"

Still in his prophetic state, Jesus foresaw the destruction that would fall on Jerusalem in less than forty years. In spite of Jerusalem's shortcomings, in spite of all that he has said, he still would have dropped everything and embraced the whole people if there had been a willingness there. But there was not.

There is the closing of a book here on Jesus' prophetic ministry. Now the direction is toward the end and his eventual triumphant return. Up until now he had held out some hope for the people's response. No more. The die was cast.

146

Matthew 24

Matthew 24:1-2

[1] Jesus left and was going away from the temple when his disciples came to him to show him the temple's buildings. [2] "Yes," he said, "you may well look at all these. I tell you this: not a single stone here will be left in its place; every one of them will be thrown down."

While this had been going on, the disciples had been sightseeing in the marvelous temple precincts for which the Jewish nation could be grateful to Herod the Great. No doubt this was the first trip to Jerusalem for most of them. And they must have shared some of the wonder of typical Holy Land pilgrims.

But Jesus was not in a mood to admire. His eyes were still focused on the destruction he saw ahead. Not a single stone would be left on the other, he said. He saw this terrible picture accurately. Before the fury of the Roman legions would have been spent some forty years hence, the city would be reduced to rubble. Some stones from Herod's magnificent temple would be dragged two and three miles down the mountain.

24:3-14

[3] As Jesus sat on the Mount of Olives, the disciples came to him in private. "Tell us when all this will be," they asked, "and what will happen to show that it is the time for your coming and the end of the age."

[4] Jesus answered, "Watch out, and do not let anyone fool you. [5] Because many men will come in my name, saying, 'I am the Messiah!' and fool many people. [6] You are going to hear the noise of battles close by and the news of battles far away; but, listen, do not be troubled. Such things must happen, but they do not mean that the end has come. [7] Countries will fight each other, kingdoms will attack one another. There will be famines and earthquakes everywhere. [8] All these things are like the first pains of childbirth.

[9] "Then you will be arrested and handed over to be punished, and be put to death. All mankind will hate you because of me. [10] Many will give up their faith at that time; they will betray each other and hate each other. [11] Then many false prophets will appear and fool many people. [12] Such will be the spread of evil that many people's love will grow cold. [13] But whoever holds out to the end will be saved. [14] And this Good News about the Kingdom will be preached through all the world, for a witness to all mankind; and then will come the end."

The disciples had come to accept Jesus' death. They were beginning to make provision for themselves between his departure and his coming again. They wished to be instructed in the ways they would know that the end was near.

The signs to which Jesus pointed are generally negative. There will be plenty more wars and bloodshed in the world. There will be people claiming to be The Messiah. Such things are not a sign of the end.

There will be an intensification of persecution. Christians will experience universal hatred. Many Christians will abandon their faith. False prophets will enjoy great followings. Evil will be appearing to win the day.

Prior to the end of the age and the return of the Messiah, a universal Christian mission will have been accomplished.

24:15-28

[15] "You will see 'The Awful Horror,' of which the prophet Daniel spoke, standing in the holy place." [Note to the reader: understand what this means!] [16] "Then those who are in Judea must run away to the hills. [17] The man who is on the roof of his house must not take the time to go down and get his belongings from the house. [18] The man who is in the field must not go back to get his cloak. [19] How terrible it will be in those days for women who are pregnant, and for mothers who have little babies! [20] Pray to God that you will not have to run away during the winter or on a Sabbath! [21] For the trouble at that time will be far more terrible than any there has ever been, from the beginning of the world to this very day. Nor will there ever be anything like it. [22] But God has already reduced the number of days; had he not done so, nobody would survive. For the sake of his chosen people, however, God will reduce the days.

[23] "Then, if anyone says to you, 'Look, here is the Messiah!' or 'There he is!' — do not believe him. [24] For false Messiahs and false prophets will appear; they will perform great signs and wonders for the purpose of deceiving God's chosen people, if possible. [25] Listen! I have told you this ahead of time.

[26] "Or, if people should tell you, 'Look, he is out in the desert!' — don't go there; or if they say, 'Look, he is hiding here!' — don't believe it. [27] For the Son of Man will come like the lightning which flashes across the whole sky from the east to the west.

[28] "Wherever there is a dead body the vultures will gather."

The location of the abomination of desolation in the Temple seems to link the end of the age with the destruction of Jerusalem. (See Daniel 11:31) People in Judea are envisioned as the main victims. The terror of those days will be almost past bearing.

More false prophets and false Messiahs will appear. They will be able to do signs and wonders, which indicates that miracle working power in itself is not sufficient to vouch for the reliability of anyone.

When the Messiah does come, one will not have to go anywhere looking for him. He will be visible to all everywhere.

24:29-31

[29] *"Soon after the trouble of those days the sun will grow dark, the moon will no longer shine, the stars will fall from heaven, and the powers in space will be driven from their courses. [30] Then the sign of the Son of Man will appear in the sky; then all the tribes of earth will weep, and they will see the Son of Man coming on the clouds of heaven with power and great glory. [31] The great trumpet will sound, and he will send out his angels to the four corners of the earth, and they will gather his chosen people from one end of the world to the other."*

The end time will include cosmic eruptions. Even the heavenly powers will be shaken. The sign of the Son of Man is not identified. Perhaps it is the cross. The Son of Man will come as he was seen in Daniel's vision (7:13) riding upon the clouds. The sound of the trumpet will be heard. And the angels will gather the chosen from every part of the world (since the gospel will have been preached in every part of the world).

24:32-35

[32] *"Let the fig tree teach you a lesson. When its branches become green and tender, and it starts putting out leaves, you know that summer is near. [33] In the same way, when you see all these things, you will know that the time is near, ready to begin. [34] Remember this! All these things will happen before the people now living have all died. [35] Heaven and earth will pass away; my words will never pass away."*

For everything there is a season; the fig tree, as all of living nature, teaches it. The world, too, has a life that it is living, and for those capable of reading the signs, it can be seen that they are moving to fulfillment.

The most problematic verse in Jesus' vision of future events is 34. As far as the normal eye can see, all of the things predicted by Jesus did not happen. It is true that many of the things expected in the end occurred. The Holy Spirit, expected for the end time by Joel, was poured out. The prophecies concerning disaster came for Jerusalem through the agency of Roman armies.

But all things did not happen. That does not mean that they will not happen. But it does seem that Jesus expected a quick unfolding and all things have not happened so quickly.

24:36-44

[36] "No one knows, however, when that day and hour will come — neither the angels in heaven, nor the son; the Father alone knows. [37] The coming of the Son of Man will be like what happened in the time of Noah. [38]Just as in the days before the Flood, people ate and drank, men and women married, up to the very day Noah went into the ark; [39] yet they did not know what was happening until the Flood came and swept them all away. That is how it will be when the Son of Man comes. [40] At that time two men will be working in the field: one will be taken away, the other will be left behind. [41] Two women will be at the mill grinding meal: one will be taken away, the other will be left behind. [42] Watch out, then, because you do not know what day your Lord will come. [43] Remember this: if the man of the house knew the time when the thief would come, he would stay awake and not let the thief break into his house. [44] For this reason, then, you also must be always ready, because the Son of Man will come at an hour when you are not expecting him."

The other side of the story is that only God the Father knows when this age will draw to a close. Many will have visions of the end, as did Daniel, Jesus, John, and many seers after them. But if it is only God who knows, none of those visions will tell the whole truth or reveal a strict timetable.

Although there are signs to be seen, the coming will be a surprise to many people. The fellow citizens of Noah would not believe there would be a flood. When they were knee deep in water it was too late.

The moral of the story is that each person and every community and nation should so conduct itself that, even if the coming is a surprise, it will not be an unwelcome surprise.

24:45-51

[45] *"Who, then, is the faithful and wise servant? He is the one whom his master has placed in charge of the other servants, to give them their food at the proper time. [46] How happy is that servant if his master finds him doing this when he comes home! [47] Indeed, I tell you, the master will put that servant in charge of all his property. [48] But if he is a bad servant, he will tell himself, 'My master will not come back for a long time,' [49] and he will begin to beat his fellow servants, and eat and drink with drunkards. [50] Then that servant's master will come back some day when he does not expect him and at a time he does not know. [51] The master will cut him to pieces, and make him share the fate of the hypocrites. There he will cry and gnash his teeth."*

Christian responsibility does not consist in speculations about the end, but in proper stewardship of this world's life and goods. Martin Luther was asked what he would do if he knew the world was going to end tomorrow. "Plant a tree today," he is said to have replied. A person who did would be like the faithful servant of verse 46 who was carrying out his regular responsibilities.

The person who takes God's delay in the fulfillment of the Kingdom as a sign of God's lack of concern and as an opportunity for living life as if there were no tomorrow cannot look forward to a bright future, but a harsh judgment.

Matthew 25

Matthew 25:1-13

[1] "On that day the Kingdom of heaven will be like ten girls who took their oil lamps and went out to meet the bridegroom. [2] Five of them were foolish, and the other five were wise. [3] The foolish ones took their lamps but did not take any extra oil with them, [4] while the wise ones took containers full of oil with their lamps. [5] The bridegroom was late in coming, so the girls began to nod and fall asleep.

[6] "It was already midnight when the cry rang out, 'Here is the bridegroom! Come and meet him!' [7] The ten girls woke up and trimmed their lamps. [8] Then the foolish ones said to the wise ones, 'Let us have some of your oil, because our lamps are going out.' [9] 'No, indeed,' the wise ones answered back, 'there is not enough for you and us. Go to the store and buy some for yourselves.' [10] So the foolish girls went off to buy some oil, and while they were gone the bridegroom arrived. The five girls who were ready went in with him to the wedding feast, and the door was closed.

[11] "Later the other girls arrived. 'Sir, sir! Let us in!' they cried. [12] 'But I really don't know you,' the bridegroom answered."

[13] And Jesus concluded, "Watch out, then, because you do not know the day or hour."

The parable of the ten maidens is another story of the relentlessness of God's judgment. The five foolish young women who were a part of the welcoming committee had not made provision for the possibility of the bridegroom's being delayed.

Those who had extra oil did not have sufficient additional supplies to lend to those who had none. Therefore, they told them to get additional supplies. When the bridegroom came, they were not present. Therefore, they did not gain entrance in the procession nor were they admitted when they returned.

The parable is a story of the necessity for preparedness. One should not look in the details of the parable as examples of other conduct. Otherwise one wonders why the five young women did not share. One wonders why the bridegroom did not ask the five young women who were present to vouch for those who were not. But secondary details like that are not important.

The point is that stated in verse 13. "Be prepared."

152

25:14-30

[14] "It will be like a man who was about to leave home on a trip; he called his servants and put them in charge of his property. [15] He gave to each one according to his ability: to one he gave five thousand dollars, to the other two thousand dollars, and to the other one thousand dollars. Then he left on his trip. [16] The servant who had received five thousand dollars went at once and invested his money and earned another five thousand dollars. [17] In the same way the servant who received two thousand dollars earned another two thousand dollars. [18] But the servant who received one thousand dollars went off, dug a hole in the ground, and hid his master's money.

[19] "After a long time the master of those servants came back and settled accounts with them. [20] The servant who had received five thousand dollars came in and handed over the five thousand dollars. 'You gave me five thousand dollars, sir,' he said. 'Look! Here are another five thousand dollars that I have earned.' [21] 'Well done, good and faithful servant!' said his master. 'You have been faithful in managing small amounts, so I will put you in charge of large amounts. come on in I will and share my happiness!' [22] Then the servant who had been given two thousand dollars came in and said, 'You gave me two thousand dollars, sir. Look! Here are another two thousand dollars that I have earned.' [23] 'Well done, good and faithful servant!' said his master. 'You have been faithful in managing small amounts, so I will put you in charge of large amounts. Come on in and share my happiness!' [24] Then the servant who had received one thousand dollars came in and said, 'Sir, I know you are a hard man: and reap harvest where you did not plant, and gather crops where you did not scatter seed. [25] I was afraid, so I went off and hid your money in the ground. Look! Here is what belongs to you.' [26] 'You bad and lazy servant!' his master said. 'You knew, did you, that I reap harvests where I did not plant, and gather crops where I did not scatter seed? [27] Well, then, you should have deposited my money in the bank, and I would have received it all back with interest when I returned. [28] Now, take the money away from him and give it to the one who has ten thousand dollars. [29] For to every one who has, even more will be given, and he will have more than enough; but the one who has nothing, even the little he has will be taken away from him. [30] As for this useless servant — throw him outside in the darkness; there he will cry and gnash his teeth."

This is the parable of the talents. A talent is a measure of money. But under the influence of this parable it has come into English as a word for skill or ability. A talent is something that one has to develop if it is to have value. To have profound musical ability, but never to play an instrument or sing, is the waste of a talent.

In this particular translation the five, two, and one

talents are translated into dollars. But the meaning is the same. The money was given by an owner to his servants to use as they saw fit. He left them no instructions. Two servants invested and increased the money. They were rewarded with increased responsibility. One servant, fearing the judgment of the master, simply hid the money he had received. He was thrown out of his job and his living.

This is how it is under God. People are given abilities and opportunities. They are to make the most of them. God is a stern taskmaster like this man. But that is not a cause for paralysis. Each person is still called to make the most of what he or she has been given. That is the way it is in God's kingdom.

25:31-46

[31] *"When the Son of Man comes as King, and all the angels with him, he will sit on his royal throne, [32] and all the earth's people will be gathered before him. Then he will divide them into two groups, just as a shepherd separates the sheep from the goats: [33] he will put the sheep at his right and the goats at his left. [34] Then the King will say to the people on his right, 'You that are blessed by my Father: come! Come and receive the kingdom which has been prepared for you ever since the creation of the world. [35] I was hungry and you fed me, thirsty and you gave me drink: I was a stranger and you received me in your homes, [36] naked and you clothed me; I was sick and you took care of me, in prison and you visited me.' [37] The righteous will then answer him, 'When, Lord, did we ever see you hungry and feed you, or thirsty and give you drink? [38] When did we ever see you a stranger and welcome you in our homes, or naked and clothe you? [39] When did we ever see you sick or in prison, and visit you?' [40] The King will answer back, 'I tell you, indeed, whenever you did this for one of the least important of these brothers of mine, you did it for me!'*

[41] 'Then he will say to those on his left, 'Away from me, you that are under God's curse! Away to the eternal fire which has been prepared for the Devil and his angels! [42] I was hungry but you would not feed me, thirsty but you would not give me drink; [43] I was a stranger but you would not welcome me in your homes, naked but you would not clothe me; I was sick and in prison but you would not take care of me.' [44] Then they will answer him, 'When, Lord, did we ever see you hungry, or thirsty, or a stranger, or naked, or sick, or in prison, and we would not help you?' [45] The King will answer them back, 'I tell you, indeed, whenever you refused to help one of these least important ones, you refused to help me.' [46] These, then, will be sent off to eternal punishment; the righteous will go to eternal life."

If one ever has cause to wonder what is a God-pleasing life, he or she need only re-read the story of the final judgment. There is nothing complicated here. Each person will be judged not by what he has said, but by how he has lived. Every person will have to appear before God's judgment seat and she will be judged by the conduct of her life.

That judgment will come as a surprise to many. Some will be surprised because they were not religious folk. They could not understand when they were told they did something for the Son of Man. But be they Christian, Jew, Hindu, or atheist, they had reached out in love to their fellow human beings.

Others will be surprised because they had been fine religious folk. They had gone to church and served as elders. They had been ministers and Sunday School teachers. But they had not had time for their fellow creatures.

In whom does the Christian see Jesus Christ in the world? According to verse 44, it is in the hungry, the thirsty, the stranger, the naked, the sick, and the prisoner. Jesus is identified with the helpless of the world. Earlier in his ministry he had said "I came to heal the sick; the well have no need of a physician." That was not a passing comment. It reflected his fundamental identification with the downtrodden of the world. And that continues to the end of time, in hundreds of thousands of Jesuses each person meets along the way.

And upon how each person responds, turns his or her fate, expressed this time in language of finality — eternal punishment or eternal life.

Matthew 26

Matthew 26:1-5

[1] When Jesus had finished teaching all these things, he said to his disciples, [2] "In two days, as you know, it will be the Feast of Passover, and the Son of Man will be handed over to be nailed to the cross."

[3] Then the chief priests and the Jewish elders met together in the palace of Caiaphas, the High Priest, [4] and made plans to arrest Jesus secretly and put him to death. [5] "We must not do it during the feast," they said, "or the people will riot."

This is the fourth prediction of his passion uttered by Jesus. The time is practically there now.

The political situation in Judah has been discussed earlier in this commentary. While Galilee in the north was governed by Herod Antipas, Herod's Judean son had not long survived. At his departure Judea had been made a military province, and a Roman governor was in charge of the government. But because Judea was something of a theocracy, a High Priest in Jerusalem and a Council of Seventy, the Sanhedrin, retained significant role in local affairs.

It is this group that first made plans for Jesus' death. It is not definite during this time whether the Jewish officials had power to execute a religious charge. Verse 4 of Matthew seems to imply that they do.

The move against Jesus is to be made on the edge of the feast because of his continuing popularity with the people.

26:6-13

[6] While Jesus was at the house of Simon the leper, in Bethany, [7] a woman came to him with an alabaster jar filled with an expensive perfume, which she poured on Jesus' head as he was eating. [8] The disciples saw this and became angry. "Why all this waste?" they asked. [9] "This perfume could have been sold for a large amount and the money given to the poor!"

[10] Jesus knew what they were saying and said to them, "Why are you bothering this woman? It is a fine and beautiful thing that she has done for me. [11] You will always have poor people with you, but I will not be with you always. [12] What she did was to pour this perfume on my body to get me ready for burial. [13] Now, remember this! Wherever this gospel is preached, all over the world, what she has done will be told in memory of her."

One of the more touching stories of the gospel is the anointing of Jesus. During the period of his ministry he had done a great deal for many people. But little had been done for him. On this occasion an unnamed woman dares an extravagant gesture as a sign of love for Jesus.

The occasion becomes one of controversy and teaching. The disciples, having been much impressed by Jesus' own concern for the poor, saw her act as a waste. The perfume could have been converted to money for the poor. It would not be surprising, if one were hearing this story for the first time, if Jesus had agreed with them.

But instead he endorsed acts of devotion. Life is not simply relentless progress, even progress for the social betterment of humankind. Life is not worth living without a tender reaching out, one person to another. That is a part of why God created life in the first place.

So an act of devotion finds its place among the hard sayings and lofty goals of the gospel. This, too, would be proclaimed as a witness to someone who knew the gospel to be tender loving care which does not count the cost.

26:14-16

[14] *Then one of the twelve disciples — the one named Judas Iscariot — went to the chief priests [15] and said, "What will you give me if I hand Jesus over to you?" They counted out thirty silver coins and gave them to him. [16] From then on Judas was looking for a good chance to betray Jesus.*

Why did Judas betray Jesus? Few characters in modern literature have been so popular as Judas. Anyone who tells the story of Jesus in modern language, whether it be **Jesus Christ Superstar** or the TV epic **Jesus of Nazareth,** wrestles with the question: Why did Judas betray Jesus?

The answer is provided in this text. He betrayed him for thirty pieces of silver. The motive was greed. In a time when a fair number of public officials have made news by taking money, it should not be a surprise.

The Bible does not provide sufficient data to write a psycho-biography of Judas. What went wrong in his upbringing or in his later life? What is told is that one of Jesus' inner circle became the instrument of his arrest at a place where the crowd would not rise to defend Jesus.

26:17-25

[17] *On the first day of the Feast of Unleavened Bread the disciples came to Jesus and asked him, "Where do you want us to get the Passover meal ready for you?"*

[18] *"Go to a certain man in the city," he said to them, "and tell him: 'The Teacher says, My hour has come; my disciples and I will celebrate the Passover at your house.'"*

[19] *The disciples did as Jesus had told them and prepared the Passover meal.*

[20] *When it was evening Jesus and the twelve disciples sat down to eat.* [21] *During the meal Jesus said, "I tell you, one of you will betray me."*

[22] *The disciples were very upset and began to ask him, one after the other, "Surely you don't mean me, Lord?"*

[23] *Jesus answered, "One who dips his bread in the dish with me will betray me.* [24] *The Son of Man will die as the Scriptures say he will, but how terrible for that man who will betray the Son of Man! It would have been better for that man if he had never been born!"*

[25] *Judas, the traitor, spoke up. "Surely you don't mean me, Teacher?" he asked.*

Jesus answered, "So you say."

The passover meal was a celebration of the deliverance from Egypt. It is still celebrated by Jews and on occasions Christians may be invited into Jewish homes to learn of this meal which is the context from which the Lord's Supper emerged. It was and still is a privilege for Jews to share the Passover in Jerusalem. Passovers celebrated elsewhere include the phrase "Next year in Jerusalem."

The home for the Passover celebration was as mysteriously available as the donkey had been earlier. In fact, Jesus prescience was working well as he neared death. As he ate he sensed that the instrument through whom Satan would betray him was with him.

Eleven disciples were genuinely shocked at the charge. Only one knew what he was talking about. Jesus must have had a vision of the scene, since he had seen the hand of the betrayer and his in the dish at the same time.

Verse 24 treats of divine destiny and human freedom.
That Jesus would die had been foreseen by the Scriptures. But that did not mean that Judas had to betray
him. There was no one with a gun to his head.

The pressure of Judas' conscience drove him from his
silence when he denied the charge. Jesus indicated by his
response that he was not convinced.

26:26-30

[26] *While they were eating, Jesus took the bread, gave a prayer of
thanks, broke it, and gave it to his disciples. "Take and eat it," he said:
"this is my body."*

[27] *Then he took the cup, gave thanks to God, and gave it to them.
"Drink it, all of you," he said; [28] "this is my blood, which seals God's
covenant, my blood poured out for many for the forgiveness of sins. [29] I
tell you, I will never again drink this wine until the day I drink the new
wine with you in my Father's Kingdom."*

[30] *Then they sang a hymn and went out to the Mount of Olives.*

The meal they shared became more than a Passover.
It became the sacrament of a new exodus, a way out of
sin. The bread that Jesus distributed is his body. The
wine is his covenantal blood, poured out for forgiveness
of sins. And finally there was a vow that Jesus would not
drink wine again until they would share in the Kingdom
of the Father.

There are three movements in the meal. The body
points to a partnership with Jesus in the present. It is
the continuing bread of his presence in the church. The
blood points to Jesus as victim and the disciples as
recipients of a forgiveness won by the shedding of blood.
The vow points to the eventual reunion of Jesus with his
disciples in the Kingdom.

26:31-35

[31] *Then Jesus said to them, "This very night all of you will run
away and leave me, because the scripture says, 'God will kill the
shepherd and the sheep of the flock will be scattered.' [32] But after I
am raised to life I will go to Galilee ahead of you."*

[33] *Peter spoke up and said to Jesus, "I will never leave you, even
though all the rest do!"*

[34] *"Remember this!" Jesus said to Peter. "Before the rooster
crows tonight you will say three times that you do not know me."*

[35] Peter answered, "I will never say I do not know you, even if I have to die with you!"
And all the disciples said the same thing.

Jesus has moved beyond anger and recriminations. He was angry at the disciples when they had been unable to heal the epileptic boy. But here he predicted the cowardice of the disciples without recriminations. He does not fail to point beyond his death to the other side, when they would reunite in Galilee.

Peter did not doubt that the rest would abandon Jesus. He would not. But Jesus had seen his betrayal in advance. He even told him how soon it would happen.

The disciples all pledged their lives. And most of them were allowed to get a second chance, and a chance to give their lives.

26:36-46

[36] Then Jesus went with his disciples to a place called Gethsemane, and he said to them, "Sit here while I go over there and pray." [37] He took with him Peter, and Zebedee's two sons. Grief and anguish came over him, [38] and he said to them, "The sorrow in my heart is so great that it almost crushes me. Stay here and watch with me."

[39] He went a little farther on, threw himself face down to the ground, and prayed, "My Father, if it is possible, take this cup away from me! But not what I want, but what you want."

[40] Then he returned to the three disciples and found them asleep; and he said to Peter, "How is it that you three were not able to watch with me for one hour? [41] Keep watch, and pray so that you will not fall into temptation. The spirit is willing, but the flesh is weak."

[42] Again a second time Jesus went away and prayed, "My Father, if this cup cannot be taken away unless I drink it, your will be done." [43] He returned once more and found the disciples asleep; they could not keep their eyes open.

[44] Again Jesus left them, went away, and prayed the third time, saying the same words. [45] Then he returned to the disciples and said, "Are you still sleeping and resting? Look! The hour has come for the Son of Man to be handed over to the power of sinful men. [46] Get up, let us go. Look, here is the man who is betraying me!"

There is no text that is so clear a revelation of Jesus' humanity as the scene in the Garden at Gethsemane, on a hill outside of Jerusalem. Because he was the Son of God, and because he had such a clear sense of his mission, people often overlook his human qualities. In this text they are impossible to miss.

He was so heavy in heart that he did not want to be alone. He brought with him Peter, James, and John for companionship and support. And he went to pray. His prayer was for release from the test that lay before him. Jesus is a good example of how to pray. He did not ask for strength or support. He put before God exactly what was on his heart. He wanted out. He wanted to go back to his earlier ministry or perhaps to the carpenter shop.

But there was also a second prayer on Jesus' lips. It was a prayer of submission. "Not what I want, Father, but what you want." Jesus did not turn from wanting to fulfill God's will. But he wanted to be sure. His second prayer in verse 42 indicated that through prayer Jesus was beginning to get direction. This time he prayed, "If this is the only way, then I'll do it."

The disciples, meanwhile, were dozing. He was sadly disappointed that they could not be nearer in his time of need. But his saying to them described his own situation, too. "The spirit is willing, but the flesh is weak." He had suffered through his own bout with doubt in a way that he had not experienced spiritual struggle since the temptation. And in this circumstance, unlike the baptism and transfiguration, there was no heavenly voice to give him reassurance. Just the growing sense of peace that many experience through prayer.

And then he was ready for the crush of the last hours. The stillness of prayer was broken by strange sounds in the night.

26:47-56

[47] *Jesus was still speaking when Judas, one of the twelve disciples, arrived. With him was a large crowd carrying swords and clubs, sent by the chief priests and the Jewish elders.* [48] *The traitor had given the crowd a signal: "The man I kiss is the one you want. Arrest him!"*

[49] *When Judas arrived he went straight to Jesus and said, "Peace be with you, Teacher," and kissed him.*

[50] *Jesus answered, "Be quick about it, friend!"*

Then they came up, arrested Jesus, and held him tight. [51] *One of those who were with Jesus drew his sword and struck at the High*

Priest's slave, cutting off his ear. [52] *Then Jesus said to him, "Put your sword back in its place, because all who take the sword will die by the sword.* [53] *Don't you know that I could call on my Father for help and at once he would send me more than twelve armies of angels?* [54] *But in that case, how could the scriptures come true that say it must happen in this way?"*

[55] *Then Jesus spoke to the crowd, "Did you have to come with swords and clubs to capture me, as though I were an outlaw? Everyday I sat down and taught in the temple, and you did not arrest me.* [56] *But all this has happened to make come true what the prophets wrote in the Scriptures."*

Then all the disciples left him and ran away.

The group involved in the arrest of Jesus is described simply as a crowd. They have been authorized by the Sanhedrin. But they are not described as the temple police.

The betrayal with a sign of affection is a particularly sad note. It was such a unique act that it has become proverbial. But betrayal by friends is an old story. When a few years earlier assassins had cut down Caesar in the Roman Senate, he was shocked to see among them a close friend and responded with his last breath, "You, too, Brutus."

Jesus did not resist his arrest. One of his companions did, cutting off the ear of the slave of the High priest. Jesus put a stop to that. Violence begets violence. The hounds of war are easier to unleash than to pen up.

Should Jesus have wanted to resist, he could have called down an army of angels. But their intervention would have prevented the unfolding of the divine drama for human salvation.

Jesus did not hesitate to chide the crowd for coming like thieves in the night. An honest leadership would have arrested him in the temple. But he also understood the entire unfolding as the fulfillment of the Scriptures.

It was when the disciples saw that Jesus' predictions were chillingly coming true, and that he would use none of his great power on his own behalf, that they abandoned him and fled. Their problem was partly cowardice, but it was partly their lack of understanding and depth. They probably would have rallied round

Jesus and had it out in the garden. But a leader who would not fight, who had power he would not use, that they still could not fully comprehend. And they disappeared into the night.

26:57-68

[57] Those who had arrested Jesus took him to the house of Caiaphas, the High Priest, where the teachers of the Law and the elders had gathered together. [58] Peter followed him from a distance, as far as the couryard of the High Priest's house. He went into the courtyard and sat down with the guards, to see how it would all come out. [59] The chief priests and the whole Council tried to find some false evidence against Jesus, to put him to death: [60] but they could not find any, even though many came up and told lies about him. Finally two men stepped forward [61] and said, "This man said, 'I am able to tear down God's temple and three days later build it back up.'"

[62] The High Priest stood up and said to Jesus, "Have you no answer to give to this accusation against you?" [63] But Jesus kept quiet. Again the High Priest spoke to him, "In the name of the living God, I now put you on oath: tell us if you are the Messiah, the Son of God."

[64] Jesus answered him, "So you say. But I tell all of you: from this time on you will see the Son of Man sitting at the right side of the Almighty, and coming on the clouds of heaven!"

[65] At this the High Priest tore his clothes and said, "Blasphemy! We don't need any more witnesses! Right here you have heard his wicked words! [66] What do you think?"

They answered, "He is guilty, and must die."

[67] Then they spat in his face and beat him; and those who slapped him [68] said, "Prophesy for us, Messiah! Guess who hit you!"

Jesus was taken to the house of the High Priest where he was tried in a special session of the Sanhedrin. Almost a certainty before the Sanhedrin had sat in judgment of Herod the Great for the execution of brigands without a trial. (This was before Herod had consolidated his power.) The fact of the trial itself indicates how seriously Jewish Law took due process. But the outcome of the trial was quite different. Herod arrived in purple and with his bodyguard of armed men. The elders were clearly frightened of his growing power. When the vote came, sixty-nine voted for acquittal and only one voted for conviction. Later when Herod had consolidated his power over the entire land, he sat in judgment over the elders. He pronounced judgment on the sixty-nine that voted for his acquital, because they had not voted their convictions. And the elder who had voted for his conviction he set free, because he was a man of courage and conviction.

This story reveals that the Sanhedrin could be corrupted. It also shows that the elders to some extent held power by permission of the military rulers. In this case a motivation for moving against Jesus was his popularity with the people, which may have made for political turmoil. But a genuine religious issue was the question of the extent to which Jesus was guilty on religious grounds.

The charge of verse 61 was probably something Jesus said. No doubt he had the power. What would make the authorities nervous about that was talking about destroying the temple. It is a little bit like talking about hijacking while sitting on an airplane.

Whether or not Jesus was the Messiah was not a matter on which to be condemned. But his answer, in which he placed himself on the right hand of God, was, in Jewish eyes, blasphemy, punishable by death. It was on this charge that he was sentenced to death, or at least the Sanhedrin came to that agreement.

The abuse of Jesus was apparently a spontaneous reaction to his claims. One either comes to believe in him or sees him as someone deluded. The Sanhedrin chose the second cause.

26:69-75

[69] *Peter was sitting outside the courtyard, when one of the High Priest's servant girls came to him and said, "You, too, were with Jesus of Galilee."*

[70] *But he denied it in front of them all. "I don't know what you are talking about," he answered,* [71] *and went on out to the entrance of the courtyard. Another servant girl saw him and said to the men there, "He was with Jesus of Nazareth."*

[72] *Again Peter denied it, and answered, "I swear that I don't know that man!"*

[73] *After a little while the men standing there came to Peter. "Of course you are one of them," they said. "After all, the way you speak gives you away!"*

[74] *Then Peter made a vow: "May God punish me if I am not telling*

the truth! I do not know that man!"

Just then a rooster crowed, [75] and Peter remembered what Jesus had told him, "Before the rooster crows, you will say three times that you do not know me." He went out and wept bitterly.

Peter had stayed near enough (58) to follow the hearing. While he did not have the courage to stay with Jesus, he did not have the heart to abandon him entirely. But he soon became involved in his own mini-trial. While sitting in the courtyard with the guards, a servant girl recognized him as one of Jesus' companions.

Peter nervously denied it. But he did not act like an innocent man. Slowly he moved toward the exit. There another saw him and repeated the same charge. "He was with Jesus of Nazareth." Again he denied it, but the guards became more interested in him. They moved over for a closer look.

Now although his words denied the conviction, his accent betrayed that he was from Galilee in the north. Peter, by now, was panicky and vowed that he did not know him.

Somewhere in the distance a rooster crowed. The words of Jesus came back to him. And he cried silently to himself.

Matthew 27

Matthew 27:1-2

[1] Early in the morning all the chief priests and the Jewish elders made their plan against Jesus to put him to death. [2] They put him in chains, took him, and handed him over to Pilate, the Roman governor.

The taking of Jesus bound to Pilate represents one more escalation of the stakes. To this point it was a Jewish issue. Now the Gentile world is brought in. The fact that the Jewish leaders brought him to Pilate represents their own judgment that he was guilty, but their apparent inability to administer capital punishment.

Pilate had a reputation as a hard governor. He governed in Judea for ten years. The length at his time, five two-year terms, indicates that he was handling his position successfully in the view of his Roman supervisors.

27:3-10

[3] When Judas, the traitor, saw that Jesus had been condemned, he repented and took back the thirty silver coins to the chief priests and the elders. [4] "I have sinned by betraying an innocent man to death!" he said.

"What do we care about that?" they answered. "That is your business!"

[5] Judas threw the money into the sanctuary and left them; then he went off and hanged himself.

[6] The chief priests picked up the money and said, "This is blood money, and it is against our Law to put it in the temple treasury." [7] After reaching an agreement about it, they used the money to buy Potter's Field, as a cemetery for foreigners. [8] That is why that field is called "Field of Blood" to this very day.

[9] Then what the prophet Jeremiah had said came true, "They took the thirty silver coins, the amount the people of Israel had agreed to pay for him, [10] and used them to buy the potter's field, as the Lord commanded me."

Judas did not have the heart of a hardened criminal. When he saw what had happened to Jesus, he repented of his deed and sought to undo it. The best he could do was to return the money. But the Sanhedrin was in no mood to return Jesus.

Judas went out and hanged himself. He recognized his sin but despaired of forgiveness. He could not believe that even what he had done could be forgiven by God. To return evil for evil is bad. But to return evil for good, as Judas had done, was a terrible weight on the conscience. Yet he could have been forgiven.

The blood money did not go back into the treasury. A field was bought for the burial of foreigners, that is, it was spent for a totally secular use. Matthew says this was predicted in Jeremiah, but the quotation cited is mainly from Zachariah 11:13.

27:11-14

[11] *Jesus stood before the Governor, who questioned him. "Are you the king of the Jews?" he asked.*

"So you say," answered Jesus. [12] *He said nothing, however, to the accusations of the chief priests and elders.*

[13] *So Pilate said to him, "Don't you hear all these things they accuse you of?"*

[14] *But Jesus refused to answer a single word, so that the Governor was greatly surprised.*

Jesus would not deny his Messiahship. Neither would he respond to charges made against him before Pilate. Pilate, who had seen much of the world, could not understand someone unwilling to fight for his life.

27:15-21

[15] *At every Passover Feast the Governor was in the habit of setting free any prisoner the crowd asked for.* [16] *At that time there was a well-known prisoner named Jesus Barabbas.* [17] *So when the crowd gathered, Pilate asked them, "Which one do you want me to set free for you? Jesus Barabbas or Jesus called the Christ?"* [18] *He knew very well that they had handed Jesus over to him because they were jealous.*

[19] *While Pilate was sitting in the judgment hall, his wife sent him a message: "Have nothing to do with that innocent man, because in a dream last night I suffered much on account of him."*

[20] *The chief priests and the elders persuaded the crowds to ask Pilate to set Barabbas free and have Jesus put to death.* [21] *But the Governor asked them, "Which one of these two do you want me to set free for you?"*

"Barabbas!" they answered.

Pilate gave the crowd a voice in the matter. Did they want the release of a famous prisoner named Jesus

Barabbas or the popular prophet Jesus called the Messiah. (It is ironic that the two had the same name.)

To have the judgment of the crowd is not the same as to be judged by one's peers. The leadership circulated among them and urged that they choose Barabbas.

Meanwhile Pilate received a message from his wife that he ought not to involve himself with Jesus, an innocent man. She had been warned in a dream. This may well account for Pilate's conduct in this trial, which does not seem that of a hardened Roman officer.

When the crowd made its wishes known, it chose Barabbas, who, according to John (18:40) was a bandit. A bandit rather than a prophet!

27:22-26

[22] *"What, then, shall I do with Jesus called the Christ?" Pilate asked them.*

"Nail him to the cross!" they all answered.

[23] *But Pilate asked, "What crime has he committed?"*

Then they started shouting at the top of their voices, "Nail him to the cross!"

[24] *When Pilate saw it was no use to go on, but that a riot might break out, he took some water, washed his hands in front of the crowd, and said, "I am not responsible for the death of this man! This is your doing!"*

[25] *The whole crowd answered back, "Let the punishment for his death fall on us and on our children!"*

[26] *Then Pilate set Barabbas free for them; he had Jesus whipped and handed him over to be nailed to the cross.*

Pilate must have been unprepared for the response to his question about what he should do with Jesus. For what reason would the Passover crowd suddenly want blood? A partial explanation is that crowds do like blood. Public executions attract large audiences. Bloody accidents clog the highways with spectators. Ghoulish movies enjoy continued popularity. The blood of another sometimes is needed to convince people that they are alive.

The crowd was in no mood to take Pilate's responsibility. When he asked them for a charge, they cried all the louder, "Crucify him."

Pilate tried to escape his decision. He feared he might have a riot if he, having whetted the crowd's appetite, did not follow through. He went through the motions of washing his hands and trying to escape responsibility since he had seen nothing worthy of death in Jesus. The crowd even claimed they would accept responsibility. But it is Pilate who was responsible in that place. His washing of his hands would not change facts. Jesus was innocent. He knew him to be innocent. And he did not carry out his obligation to pronounce him innocent.

So he set Barabbas free. And he commanded that Jesus be whipped and crucified.

27:27-31

[27] Then Pilate's soldiers took Jesus into the governor's palace, and the whole company gathered around him. [28] They stripped off his clothes and put a scarlet robe on him. [29] then they made a crown out of thorny branches and placed it on his head, and put a stick in his right hand; then they knelt before him and made fun of him. "Long live the King of the Jews!" they said. [30] They spat on him, and took the stick and hit him over the head. [31] When they had finished making fun of him, they took the robe off and put his own clothes back on him. Then they led him out to nail him to the cross.

The mocking of Jesus by the soldiers of Pilate was a cruel sport enjoyed by men who did not have enough to do. It was carried on in mock seriousness, as the clothing of Jesus in a royal garment and the making of a crown suggest.

The sentence of crucifixion was a standard execution for non-Romans. It was a cruel death, designed to be an example to other would-be criminals. In the capture of Jerusalem in A.D. 70, the Romans crucified many of the city's defenders. Josephus, a Jewish general who had abandoned the war before its end, came to the city after its capture and managed to have some of his friends among those who had been crucified, taken down. One or two recovered but the rest died from the severity of the experience.

It is clear that Jesus was already in a profoundly weakened condition before he was ever placed on the cross.

27:32-44

[32] *As they were going out they met a man from Cyrene named Simon, and they forced him to carry Jesus' cross. [33] They came to a place called Golgotha, which means "The Place of the Skull." [34] There they offered him wine to drink, mixed with gall; after tasting it, however, he would not drink it.*

[35] *They nailed him to the cross, and then divided his clothes among them by throwing dice. [36] After that they sat there and watched him. [37] Above his head they put the written notice of the accusation against him: "This is Jesus, the King of the Jews." [38] Then, they nailed two bandits to crosses with Jesus, one on his right and the other on his left.*

[39] *People passing by shook their heads and hurled insults at Jesus: [40] "You were going to tear down the temple and build it back up in three days! Save yourself, if you are God's Son! Come on down from the cross!"*

[41] *In the same way the chief priests and the teachers of the Law and the elders made fun of him: [42] He saved others but he cannot save himself! Isn't he the King of Israel? If he will come down off the cross now, we will believe in him! [43] He trusts in God and says he is God's Son. Well, then, let us see if God wants to save him now!"*

[44] *Even the bandits who had been crucified with him insulted him in the same way.*

The impressing of Simon of Cyrene into service was standard Roman army practice. It underlines the fact that Jesus was too weak to handle it himself. The place of execution was a familiar spot for such occasions, as evidenced by the name. The wine offered him may have been a sedative to deaden the pain slightly. But the addition of vinegar makes it sound like Psalms 69:21.

The gambling over his clothing is anticipated by Psalms 22:18. The personal effects of the prisoner fall to the executioners.

Jesus was not alone in his suffering. Above him he had a sign indicating his title. And on each side he had bandits. People streamed by and mocked him. Those who had sought his death were emboldened by his helplessness. There is a common theme: If one has power, it ought to be used to save one's own skin. "Look out for number one." People mistook help for the world for helplessness.

Even those crucified with Jesus joined in insulting him. Matthew knows nothing about a repentant thief.

170

27:45-56

[45] *At noon the whole country was covered with darkness, which lasted for three hours. [46] At about three o'clock Jesus cried out with a loud shout, "Eli, Eli, lema sabachthani?" which means, "My God, my God, why did you abandon me?"*

[47] *Some of the people standing there heard him and said, "He is calling for Elijah!" [48] One of them ran up at once, took a sponge, soaked it in cheap wine, put it on the end of a stick, and tried to make him drink it. [49] But the others said, "Wait, let us see if Elijah is coming to save him!"*

[50] *Jesus again gave a loud cry, and breathed his last.*

[51] *Then the curtain hanging in the temple was torn in two, from top to bottom. The earth shook, the rocks split apart, [52] the graves broke open, and many of God's people who had died were raised to life. [53] They left the graves; and after Jesus rose from death they went into the Holy City, where many people saw them.*

[54] *When the army officer and the soldiers with him who were watching Jesus saw the earthquake and everything else that happened, they were terrified and said, "He really was the Son of God!"*

[55] *There were many women there, looking on from a distance, who had followed Jesus from Galilee and helped him. [56] Among them were Mary Magdalene, Mary the mother of James and Joseph, and the mother of Zebedee's sons.*

The darkness that accompanied the death of Jesus was one of the cosmic signs expected in the end time. At the conclusion of the darkness, Jesus screamed and what was heard was something like the mixture of Hebrew and Aramaic. Matthew understood him to be saying, "My God, my God, why did you abandon me?" The Gospel of Peter understood him to say, "My power, my power, you have left me."

The meaning of this phrase is murky. His hearers understood him to be calling the prophet Elijah, who was expected at the end time. Some commentators saw that he was simply reciting Psalms 22, which ends on a note of confidence. Perhaps he was just feeling the absence of God, a divine abandonment that prevented the death of the Son of God from being a charade.

After a second attempt to give Jesus wine, he gave a cry and died. The death of the Son of God was noted by heaven and earth. The temple veil — separating the Holy of Holies from the outer part — was torn from top to bottom. There was an earthquake. Even the general resurrection of the dead was anticipated by the raising of many who appeared in Jerusalem. It was likely that this was simply a temporary phenomenon rather than a permanent situation. The centurion and his men who had earlier made sport of Jesus now were properly sobered: "He really was the Son of God."

None of Jesus' disciples were nearby, according to this description. But he was not devoid of followers. A number of women, who had been a source of Jesus' material support, were near. Among them were Mary Magdalene, Mary the mother of James and Joseph (and perhaps the mother of Jesus), and the mother of James and John. The women did not abandon him just because it looked as if hope were lost.

27:57-61

[57] *When it was evening, a rich man from Arimathea arrived; his name was Joseph, and he also was a disciple of Jesus. [58] He went into the presence of Pilate and asked for the body of Jesus. Pilate gave orders for the body to be given to Joseph. [59] So Joseph took it, wrapped it in a new linen sheet, [60] and placed it in his own grave, which he had just recently dug out of the rock. Then he rolled a large stone across the entrance to the grave and went away. [61] Mary Magdalene and the other Mary were sitting there, facing the grave.*

It seems that there was always someone to help Jesus when he needed it. The donkey had been provided. So had a room for the Passover in a crowded city. A woman had anointed him for burial. Simon had carried his cross. Now even in death someone appeared to provide a tomb.

The tomb was in the side of a hill, carved out of rock. Many tombs of that period were designed like sleeping cars on a train. Two women of Jesus' company were watching that operation too, Mary Magdalene and one of the two Marys who had been at the cross.

27:62-66

[62] *On the next day — that is, the day following Friday — the chief priests and the Pharisees met with Pilate [63] and said, "Sir, we remember that while that liar was still alive he said, 'I will be raised to*

life after three days.' [64] Give orders, then, for the grave to be safely guarded until the third day, so that his disciples will not be able to go and steal him, and then tell the people, 'He was raised from death.' This last lie would be even worse than the first one."

[65] "Take a guard," Pilate told them; "go and guard the grave as best you can."

[66] So they left, and made the grave secure by putting a seal on the stone and leaving the guard on watch.

The talk of a resurrection from the dead had been enough to make some people nervous. According to the story, they were not afraid that he would be raised but that his disciples would steal the body and claim that he was raised.

So a guard was set with the cooperation of Pilate.

Matthew 28

Matthew 28:1-8

[1] After the Sabbath, as Sunday morning was dawning, Mary Magdalene and the other Mary went to look at the grave. [2] Suddenly there was a strong earthquake; an angel of the Lord came down from heaven, rolled the stone away, and sat on it. [3] His appearance was like lightning and his clothes were white as snow. [4] The guards were so afraid that they trembled and became like dead men.

[5] The angel spoke to the women. "You must not be afraid," he said, "I know you are looking for Jesus, who was nailed to the cross. [6] He is not here; he has been raised, just as he said. Come here and see the place where he lay. [7] Quickly, now, go and tell his disciples, 'He has been raised from death, and now he is going to Galilee ahead of you; there you will see him!' Remember what I have told you."

[8] So they left the grave in a hurry, afraid and yet filled with joy, and ran to tell his disciples.

[9] Suddenly Jesus met them and said, "Peace be with you." They came up to him, took hold of his feet, and worshiped him. [10] "Do not be afraid," Jesus said to them. "Go and tell my brothers to go to Galilee, and there they will see me."

A human guard did not foil the resurrection. An angel appeared who frightened the guards almost to death. He assured the women that Jesus was already gone, as he had predicted. He commissioned them to tell the good news to the disciples, which they speedily did. It was not simply a message of resurrection, but of reunion in Galilee. Just so, the joyful message at a funeral is not so much "he will live again" but "you shall meet again."

The women had not gone far before they met Jesus himself. It is as if it were a reward for their perseverance, even in the face of death. The message was the same as the angel had given them, but how great must have been the joy to hear it from his lips.

28:11-15

[11] While the women went on their way, some of the soldiers guarding the grave went back to the city and told the chief priests everything that had happened. [12] The chief priests met with the elders and made their plan; they gave a large sum of money to the soldiers [13] and said, "You are to say that his disciples came during the night and stole his body while you were asleep. [14] And if the Governor should hear of this, we will convince him and you will have nothing to worry about."

174

[15] The guards took the money and did what they were told to do. To this very day that is the report spread around by the Jews.

The news did not remain only with the followers of Jesus. The soldiers, too, had a story to tell, if only of a frightening angel and an empty tomb. According to Matthew, they were given a bribe to keep their mouths shut about wnat happened and to tell instead another story.

Those who had opposed Jesus in his life sought to discredit the story of his resurrection. But they were as little successful then as they are today.

28:16-20

[16] The eleven disciples went to the hill in Galilee where Jesus had told them to go. [17] When they saw him they worshiped him, even though some of them doubted. [18] Jesus drew near and said to them, "I have been given all authority in heaven and on earth. [19] Go, then, to all peoples everywhere and make them my disciples: baptize them in the name of the Father, the Son, and the Holy Spirit. [20] and teach them to obey everything I have commanded you. And remember! I will be with you always, to the end of the age."

The reaction of the disciples is the reaction of the church. All worshiped, some doubted. They had been part of an event that was unique in the history of the world.

But Jesus was not caught up in the mystery. He had business to do. With this small band he launched a worldwide mission. It is his will that everyone be his disciple, not for his glory but to the glory of God. It is his will that everyone be baptized in the name of the Father, the Son, and the Holy Spirit. And it is his will that his teaching concerning the Kingdom of God help shape it in the lives and among the people who receive the teaching.

Finally, the best news was that he would never leave again. Whatever tasks, whatever perils, whatever joys, whatever opportunities — they would not be faced alone. Because, said Jesus, "I am with you always."